Hamlyn all-colour paperbacks

House Plants

Joan Compton

illustrated by Henry Barnett

Hamlyn
London · New York · Sydney · Toronto

FOREWORD

The culture of house plants has a fascination entirely of its own. Unlike outdoor gardening, the work is not dependent upon weather conditions, nor is time taken up by irksome, seldom enjoyed, tasks such as mowing, weeding, sweeping, hedge-clipping, digging and staking. One does not feel the urge to rush into the garden on a wet, windy day to put sheltering arms around favourite plants, which will undoubtedly have reached perfection at that moment. House plants are untroubled by most outdoor conditions and can be enjoyed to the full, provided they are not over-watered, given a too dry atmosphere, overheated, scorched by strong sunlight or low humidity, all factors caused by carelessness and lack of thought. There is more time available to enjoy plants grown in this way because less time need be spent on the tasks that are always demanding attention outdoors. Those who grow their plants indoors can grow varieties originating from many parts of the world, thus adding yet another pleasant aspect to the entertaining pastime of indoor gardening.

J.C.

The artist wishes to acknowledge gratefully the help given by the following, who provided facilities and often actual plants for making the illustrations: Margaret Jones, Elm Garden Nurseries, Claygate, Surrey; Thomas Rochford's of Turnford Nurseries, Hoddesdon, Herts; George Wells, Foreman of the glasshouses at the Royal Horticultural Society's garden at Wisley, Surrey; the staff of the Library and Herbarium at Kew Gardens; Christina Beaven, Ranelagh Avenue, Barnes; Syon Park Garden Centre, Brentford.

Published by The Hamlyn Publishing Group Limited
London · New York · Sydney · Toronto
Astronaut House, Feltham, Middlesex, England

Phototypeset by Filmtype Services Limited, Scarborough
Colour separations by Schwitter Limited, Zurich
Printed in Spain by Mateu Cromo, Madrid

CONTENTS

INTRODUCTION

The cultivation of house plants to decorate today's homes is very popular. Practical books that give advice and information on the choice of plants, their daily care, and the way in which they can best be displayed are now essential to novice and beginner alike.

People in all walks of life have always grown house plants, from geraniums on cottage windowsills to potted palms in Victorian conservatories. Their history goes back for many generations, and has been told too often to be repeated here. No doubt the fact that the western world is rapidly becoming more urbanized and there are fewer gardens in which to potter, urges most of us to express that inherent love of growing things, deeply rooted by a long tradition of civilization. Now, although we have no garden, it is still possible to grow, as our forebears did, many decorative and interesting plants for the home. Many more and greater varieties can be obtained, for larger windows, central heating, the disappearance of gas lighting, the fumes from which were always anathema to living plants, and the greater choice of plants now available at quite reasonable prices, all encourage us to try our hands at this rewarding hobby. Cut flowers can provide a very decorative note in any room, but it is necessarily a temporary one only. Cut flowers cannot give the same sense of achievement either, for immense satisfaction can be obtained from watching the gradual transformation of a small plant to a healthy full-grown specimen.

In most ways, indoor gardening is preferable to outdoor. Rain, wind, gales and frost impede progress outside, whereas an indoor routine can be established without worrying about what is going on outside the window. Plants in pots are mobile too. They can be moved around to alter the background completely. More sun, less sun, higher or lower levels, a group instead of a marshalled row, a mixed bowl or a trough, all give fresh interest and the variety is endless. There should be no time to spend regretting the gardens of former times.

This is modern gardening. The ways in which plants can be displayed in various settings, such as offices, hospitals, shop windows, conference rooms, commercial premises and hotels, are limitless but in domestic surroundings the plants are part of the home and should share their position with the owners and with the furniture, whether period or contemporary, to make a harmonious whole. This is why so many chosen house plants are green, for this colour blends so well with all other colours. If there are brightly coloured curtains or upholstery, however, one should not forget to consider them when choosing a plant with coloured flowers, leaves or berries.

A sunroom or conservatory is a room for plants and there they can have their own way, for the colours of nature seldom clash. To anyone who is bound to their flat by illness or old age, the growing of indoor plants gives a constant interest. Just one pot of something growing can give so much pleasure. The owner has constant interest, a responsibility for the care of the plant and a delight in its well-being that is very satisfying. This book covers a wide range of house plants. Plants that will stand the worst possible conditions are included as well as others that can be grown with adequate warmth and humidity. No plant can be treated as an ornament and, for those who are prepared to spare a little time, growing house plants can be an absorbing pastime.

CHOOSING HOUSE PLANTS

The choice of plants is very wide, but for the beginner it is wiser to start with a few hardy plants; to gradually become used to their requirements, the diseases which may attack them, the amount of water they need at various times of the year and the feeding they may require. It is useless to choose plants for appearance only, for choice must primarily depend on the growing conditions required. Later, choice widens with experience and eventually one is able to deal with any plant, no matter how delicate. Hardy plants have a certain tolerance for fluctuating temperatures and can overlook neglect in matters such as watering and feeding for short periods.

An ability to thrive in shady conditions is essential for some plants, because the light that they get indoors approximates to their natural habitat, the forests of Malaysia or tropical South America, from which the vast majority of house plants originate. It is not usually possible to give ideal growing conditions for plants in a room primarily adjusted to the needs of personal living. Even well-lighted rooms are shady in comparison with open conditions in gardens and, as light enters a room mainly through its windows, its intensity and duration depends on their aspect. Temperatures are mainly a winter problem. The level at night is crucial; the minimum temperature that should be consistently maintained should be 50°F, although a number of plants can strive in a temperature of 5° less. This is fairly easy to maintain and, if there is central heating, it may often be exceeded.

A dry atmosphere causes moisture loss from leaves, roots, and soil which must be offset by creating more humidity around the plants. One of the easiest ways to increase humidity is to put the plant pot into another, larger, container and to fill the extra space between outside container and inner pot with something absorbent, such as peat, which can be kept permanently moist. Some plants do, however, prefer a dry atmosphere. Among them are *Sansevieria*, *Pittosporum, Sedum, Grevillea* and *Aspidistra*. Plants that appreciate a dry atmosphere usually like as much light as possible. All house plants should be removed before a room is painted, although most are unaffected by tobacco smoke.

Sedum

Sansevieria
trifasciata laurenti

Aspidistra lurida

Grevillea
robusta

(From left to right) Fatsia japonica, Chlorophytum elatum variegatum, Cissus antarctica

HOUSE PLANTS FOR SPECIAL REQUIREMENT$

Hardy house plants

The following hardy plants are all suitable for the beginner. They are decorative, are capable of thriving in fluctuating temperatures, provided they are not subject to frost, and are capable of standing up to erratic watering.

Aspidistra lurida is a tolerant, easily grown house plant. Known in America as the Cast Iron Plant, its tough, long, lanceolate leaves grow in sheaves. A well grown plant may occasionally flower, but the small purple bells are inconspicuous and it is for the dark green, glossy leaves this plant is grown. It is tolerant of fumes, indifferent to changes in temperature and survives in either light or shade.

Chlorophytum elatum variegatum (Spider Plant) will thrive in the most unlikely places in the house, but it needs a fair amount of light. It is a native of South Africa and has long, narrow, linear leaves that are smooth, green and white. The flower spikes carry small tufts of leaves which will root easily in the summer, if pegged on small pots adjacent to the parent plant.

Cissus antarctica (Kangaroo Vine) has been a pioneer among house plants and is very popular in Scandinavia as a climber. It will thrive happily a few feet away from the window and support itself by its tendrils. It is first class for an indoor trellis.

Cissus capensis from South America is equally vigorous, but more trailing in growth. It has kidney-shaped, toothed leaves and likes a light position, but not direct sun. *C. striata,* from Chile, may be grown as a bushy trailer, *C. socyoides,* also from tropical South America, is a more vigorous climber.

Fatsia japonica, an evergreen shrub from Japan, is tolerant of shade and excellent for cool rooms and halls. It has stout stems and large, leathery leaves, palmately cut.

Ficus elastica decora is the India-rubber Plant of tropical Asia, and the easiest member of the family to grow. It has a thick woody stem and stiff, dark green leaves with red touches when unfolding.

Grevillea robusta from Australia has fern-like, silky, bronze-green leaves, which contrast well with other more solid house plants. It needs moderate watering, increasing as the temperature rises.

Ficus elastica decora, the India-rubber Plant *(above)* and *Cissus capensis (below)*

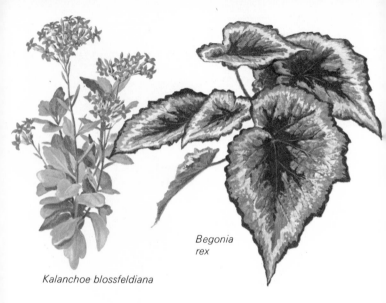

Begonia
rex

Kalanchoe blossfeldiana

Plants requiring minimum temperature 10° – 12°C
These plants require more care than those given in the first
list because they are more tender and need more consistent
watering and attention.

Begonia rex is a rhizomatous plant, grown for its decorative
leaves. The flowers are relatively small and can be removed
to strengthen leaf growth. The leaves are radical, obliquely
oval in shape, with a heart-shaped base tapering to a point.
B. masoniana (Iron Cross) is another foliage begonia, originally
from Singapore. The grey-green leaves have a moss-covered
appearance and a large brownish cross-shaped zone in the
centre. Both plants like humidity away from direct sunlight.

Beloperone guttata (Shrimp Plant), from Mexico, makes a small
shrub suitable for a house plant, up to 2 feet in height. It has
soft, shining, green, oval leaves and terminal arching spikes
of flowers that are almost hidden by brownish-pink, overlapping bracts with some resemblance to a shrimp. It is easily
grown and likes plenty of sun and light.

Billbergia nutans from Brazil, grows with rosettes of narrow,
grass-like, silvery green leaves about a foot long. The flowers
are a drooping spike made up of rose-pink bracts surrounding

Peperomia caperata (left) and *Begonia masoniana (right)*

small flowers, appearing in late winter and early spring.

Codiaeum variegatum pictum (Croton) is a native of Malaya. House plant specimens are pot grown to a single stem, up to 2 feet high, with smooth leathery leaves marked in vivid colours. The plants are exacting in their requirements; ample light, high humidity, an even temperature and watering and syringing in summer, less in winter.

Euphorbia splendens, a native of Madagascar, is popularly known as the 'Crown of Thorns' because the branching brown stems are beset with long tapering spines. A few small green leaves appear on the tips of the branches, and small flowers, each enclosed in a pair of blood-red bracts, are borne in clusters from winter until early summer. While in flower they should be watered moderately, decreasing the amount as flowers and bracts fade.

Kalanchoe are half-hardy succulent plants, found in tropical and southern Africa. They have showy, attractively coloured leaves, and *K. blossfeldiana* is probably the most successful house plant. Growing 12 inches high, it produces many stems with dark green notched leaves edged with red and panicles of small orange-red flowers, scented in the winter months.

Monstera deliciosa, a native of Mexico, grows with erect stiffish stems, which are better for some support, as it is a creeper rather than a climber. The leaves are broadly ovate, tough, leathery and dark green with a deeply incised edge and large holes in the leaf blade. In America it is known as the Ceriman, and in nature bears a spadix of yellowish flowers that give way to edible fruits with a pineapple flavour. It is far too large for most rooms, for its leaves can be 4 feet long and 2 feet across but smaller varieties can be obtained. Monsteras are slow growers and may be grown in large pots, watering with care as too much or too little can cause yellowing at the leaf tips. They are good plants for halls and foyers.

Nephrolepis exaltata is a tropical fern with finely cut, pinnate, green fronds of up to 2 feet long and 6 inches broad, a rapid grower which needs a fair amount of room. *N. cordifolia compacta* is also excellent for pots, with deep green, glossy, arching fronds, about 2 feet long. Both of these ferns like shade and liberal watering in summer, more moderate watering in winter. Propagation is by division in March.

Peperomia caperata is one of the many members of the *Peperomia* genus, which has some 400 species, all of American origin. *P. caperata* is a dwarfish plant with oval tapering

Codiaeum or Croton *(left)*
Scindapsus 'Marble Queen' *(below)*

12

leaves of dark corrugated green and white, taper-like spikes of flowers in season. *P. hederaefolia* has silvery markings. They need light, airy conditions without draughts and only moderate watering, even more sparingly in winter.

Scindapsus aureus requires a certain amount of light to keep its colour, but too strong sunlight will burn the leaves. The variety 'Marble Queen' has creamy-white foliage flecked with green and is a good contrast plant to grow in a green setting.

Sedum sieboldii from Japan, an easily grown plant, is only of annual duration. At the end of autumn it will die down and will not start into growth again until late spring. Before dying down, the plant produces heads of pink flowers. When growing the plant likes light, but little water. When growth is complete, water should be withheld altogether and plants kept dry, then given a good soak to restart growth.

Zebrina pendula is a pleasing, easily grown house plant, native to the southern United States and Mexico. The narrow, oval leaves are 2 inches long, coloured with a central green stripe, with silver, purple and dark green to the edges, and purple-red below. Plants need a light airy position, and should be watered freely in summer, moderately in winter. Pinching back in spring induces bushiness.

Peperomia hederaefolia (above) and Beloperone guttata (right)

Plants requiring minimum temperature 12°–15°C

Aphelandra squarrosa louisae is of Brazilian origin and grows erectly with large, lance-shaped, dark green leaves. The central and lateral veins are etched in white and droop in opposite pairs down the upright stem. From the top pair arises a bright yellow flower spike about 2 inches in length. The spikes must be cut out after flowering just above the nearest pair of leaves. Aphelandras require a warm situation, with plenty of light, but protection from direct sunlight. The leaves must be sprayed daily, or sponged weekly with a damp sponge. They need to be pot-bound to flower well.

Begonia boweri is a small begonia from Mexico, with a creeping rhizome. It grows a few inches high and its leaves seldom exceed 3 inches in length. The leaves are emerald green with a narrow, maroon-coloured zone around the edge. It should be treated as *B. rex* (page 10) but will tolerate more light.

Caladium are characterized by having tuberous rhizomes for roots. The beautiful leaves are in a variety of colours and die down each winter and reappear in spring. They need a fair amount of heat to bring them to perfection. The chief species

Fittonia verschaeffeltii rubra (below) and (right) Aphelandra squarrosa louisae

14

Cissus discolor

Dracaena fragrans

are *C. bicolor*, which has green and red leaves, *C. picturatum*, green and yellow and *C. schomburgkii* green, white and silver, but as they cross-fertilize readily there are many hybrids. These plants must have high temperature and humidity and water must be gradually withheld as the leaves fade. The dormant tubers can be stored in their pots.

Cissus discolor is a very attractive plant, although it tends to shed many of its leaves in winter. It is naturally a climber and makes a good plant for a hanging basket. Summer temperature should ideally be 18° C.

Diffenbachia are erect evergreen perennials native to tropical America, that make effective foliage plants for the house where a minimum temperature of 13° C can be consistently maintained. Growth should be kept as continuous as possible as the individual leaves do not survive for a long period. The plants are commonly known as 'Dumb Canes' and are extremely poisonous. Biting any part of them will prevent speech for several days. *D. bowmannii* develops very large, wavy-edged leaves of deep green, with light green markings, up to 2 feet long and 12 inches across. There are others, mostly smaller, such as *D. picta* from Brazil, with dark green, long, pointed leaves spotted with pale green, white or cream.

15

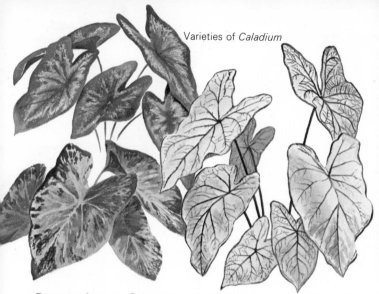

Dracaena fragrans from tropical Africa are grown for their foliage, which consists of long sword-like leaves. *D. sanderiana* is a smaller slender plant with green leaves 6 to 9 inches long, $1\frac{1}{2}$ inches wide, with a broad white margin. All varieties enjoy semi-shade, a warm humid atmosphere, and leaves sponged frequently.

Fittonia are perennial Peruvian evergreens that are distinctive for their marked and netted foliage. There are only three species. *F. argyroneura* is a dwarf trailing plant, with heart-shaped oval leaves 3 to 4 inches long and 2 to 3 inches wide, which are netted with ivory-white veins. On *F. verschaffeltii* the ground colour is dark green and the veins are red. The third species, *F. gigantea,* grows to a height of 18 inches with broad ovate leaves and carmine-red veins. All species need warmth, shade and humidity and should be watered and sprayed freely in summer. The flowers are insignificant, and should be pinched out.

Peperomia magnoliaefolia is a sturdy shrubby plant with compact growth and frequent side shoots. The leaves are an elongated oval shape about 2 inches long and about $1\frac{3}{4}$ inches wide and have an attractive glossy appearance throughout their lives. 'Green Gold' is a variety of recent introduction. The leaves are edged and splashed with creamy-yellow, the centres streaked with greyish-green. They like light, airy conditions, no draughts and only moderate watering in summer, more sparingly in winter.

Pilea cadieri (Aluminium Plant) is an extremely popular house plant. The leaves are long-stalked, oblong-oval in shape with a slightly toothed edge. They are dark green with silvery patches between the veins. It needs light, airy conditions, regular watering and feeding in summer and minimum watering in winter.

Platycerium (Stag's Horn Fern) is an extraordinary epiphytic fern that has recently become very popular as a house plant. It is found in many warm countries, including Australia, and is distinguished by bifurcated and forking fertile fronds. The easiest to grow indoors is *P. bifurcatum*. It can be attached vertically to a piece of cork bark, the roots covered by a mixture of equal parts of fibrous peat and *Sphagnum* moss and held in place by copper wire. To water, the root ball and bark can be soaked for a few minutes and left to drain before rehanging.

Diffenbachia picta

Peperomia magnoliaefolia 'Green Gold'

Echeveria and two
varieties of *Aloe*

Plants for sunny windowsills

These are plants that need ample light, although no plant should be subjected to direct hot sunlight through glass. A light curtain or blind should be drawn to shield them from the direct rays of summer sun, or the plants can be moved further into the room and put back on the sill later in the day when the sun has lost its midday heat.

Agave (American Aloe) make attractive foliage plants for the house when young, as they are easy to grow. They welcome the brightest of light, but become too large for small windowsills eventually and the stout spines on the leaves become a hazard. Of the smaller species, *A. albicans* from Mexico, is perhaps the best, with small rosettes of broad whitish leaves, edged with horny teeth. Plants may be placed out of doors in pots in summer.

Aloe are evergreen succulent plants, native to South Africa. There are several species attractive for their fleshy leaves and popular for their hardiness under fluctuating indoor conditions. *A. variegata*, the Partridge-breasted Aloe, with its dark green leaves, banded with white markings, and upright spike of pale orange tubular flowers, is well worth growing.

Echeveria is a genus of about 150 succulents that originated in the south and west of North America. *E. setosa* is one of the most decorative varieties with low rosettes of pointed leaves, closely covered with soft white bristles. Showy, red-tipped, yellow flowers appear in summer.

Hoya carnosa comes from Queensland, Australia. It is an ever-green climbing plant, capable of growing up to 10 feet and easily managed, becoming more attractive with age. It is best trained up a trellis or a support by a window, but can also be grown as a trailer. The leaves are dark green, somewhat fleshy, oval and pointed. The starry flowers are fragrant and bloom for several weeks in spring and summer. It needs a summer temperature of 13° to 18°C with liberal watering and a winter temperature of about 10°C and very moderate watering.

Impatiens hybrids, which most people know as Busy Lizzies, are seldom out of flower, even in the winter months. They like a light, airy, summer position, liberal watering and occasional pinching out of shoots to keep plants bushy. The taller kinds benefit from staking, for their stems are very brittle. They flower well in quite small pots and benefit from being syringed in summer months and being kept fairly dry in winter. Propagation is by cuttings.

Impatiens or Busy Lizzie

Plants for hall or staircase

The entrance hall is one of the most important points in the scheme of house or apartment planning and needs to convey a pleasant atmosphere of welcome. It is probably rather dark and, although the use of house plants will help to make the entrance hall more inviting, it is important to remember that draughts can have a lethal effect on many plants and also that variegated foliage will lose its variegation, unless it has ample light.

Aspidistra lurida (page 7) would seem to be a good plant for this situation and the variety *variegata* is really more interesting, with alternate green and white striping on the leaves, but it needs more light than is often available here.

Monstera deliciosa, if there is sufficient space, makes a handsome plant for a foyer or a hall. Its large, leathery, green leaves which reach up to 2 feet across and are deeply cut or perforated, are not affected by shade. Although they need a warm hall or foyer and ample watering and spraying in

A mixed planting of
Spathiphyllum wallisii
and *Sansevieria*

summer, with moderate watering in winter, they will make an imposing feature.

Sansevieria trifasciata laurentii has long, sword-like, pointed leaves, which have given rise to the unkind name of 'Mother-in-Law's Tongue'. There are various shades of green with stripes of golden-yellow and they can reach 36 inches tall. This is another plant impervious to shade.

Spathiphyllum wallisii is another attractive plant for a shady corner and one of the few house plants grown for its flowers rather than its leaves. The leaves are a bright shiny green, long and lance-shaped with a thin point at the top. The flowers, not unlike *Anthurium* in shape, appear in spring and again in autumn. They are green at first, then turn white, and then turn green again. It should be treated as delicate, but it is not unreasonable in its requirements. It likes constant shade and the leaves will turn yellowish if exposed to too bright a light. It is a rapid grower and demands plenty of water and rather more feeding than most plants even during the winter and needs frequent repotting. Red Spider is sometimes a pest. Propagation is by division.

Monstera deliciosa

KINDS OF HOUSE PLANTS
Annuals to grow in the house

This is a section that, although it contains the names of many popular plants, gives one only temporary plants for the home. Their raising takes quite a lot of time and space and the latter is not always easy to find in a flat, even if the former is possible.

Growing seed in the house is a stimulating experience and it is certainly rewarding for a novice if success follows the first efforts. The basic treatment is similar for all annuals and their main requirements in all cases are warmth, moisture and air. They are best sown in pots and afterwards pricked out in boxes. The normal seed box holds thirty-six seedlings, far too many for the average house or flat, so several kinds of plants could be pricked out in the same box. Pre-packed compost mixtures are available from all garden stores.

Bottom heat can be provided, if required, by placing seed pan or pots on a tray of moist gravel on a moderately hot radiator. Great attention must be paid to cleanliness and 'crocking', seed pans or pots are then filled with compost and lightly firmed down to a level of 1 inch below the top. The soil should be given a good soaking so that no further watering will be necessary before the seed has germinated. Small seeds

'Tom Thumb' nasturtiums *(left)* and *Primula obconica (below)*

Petunias *(top), Exacum affine (left)* and *(right) Thunbergia alata* or 'Black-eyed Susan'

can be scattered thinly and require no covering; large hard skinned seeds should be soaked in tepid water for twenty-four hours before sowing and tough skinned seeds notched with a nail file. Large seeds should be sown at a depth of at least twice their diameter.

Once seedlings have become fairly sizeable they can be potted up and, if possible, the plants put outside in a shaded position after potting, although they should be brought indoors if frost is likely. It is not possible to give too much light in winter and the usual precautions against over-watering must be taken. Plants that flower in the winter or spring like to be in well-lit positions; summer and autumn flowering plants can take a little more shade.

Calendula (Marigold) are hardy plants that grow in all soils, in sunny or shady positions. *C. officinalis* is the species that is usually cultivated and there are numerous varieties.

Cobea scandens is an attractive climber, with pale green bell-like flowers turning to purple on reaching maturity. It can reach from 10 to 30 feet.

Mimulus

Salpiglossis

Exacum affine is one of the most delightful of the small annuals, on account of its delicious scent, but it needs some heat to ensure germination of the seeds. These are very small and should be sown in spring at a temperature of 15°C. With a moderately shady position, they start flowering in late summer and continue bearing their lilac-coloured, salver-shaped flowers for about eight weeks.

Ipomea, the glorious blue 'Morning Glory', can be raised from seed, six in a 5 inch pot, later thinned to three plants. They should be given some support on which to climb.

Mimulus were once grown widely on cottage windowsills because of the lovely scent but are seldom seen nowadays, no doubt because the perfume has mysteriously disappeared. However, there are quite a number of species still available which are well worth growing as pot plants. The flowers are trumpet-shaped and are distinguished by their beautiful markings. *Mimulus moschatus* has yellow flowers, *M. luteus*, yellow spotted with brown and *M. luteus tigrinus*, tiger-like markings and spots of crimson and maroon on a yellow ground. All of these are ideal for light positions and are easily grown, only requiring a fair amount of water.

Nasturtium plants will sprout in a pot in a dim corner and then become a blaze of colour on a sunny windowsill, but either the compact 'Tom Thumb' type should be sown, or a firm pinching

Nemesia
varieties

hand kept on climbers. Pinching out tops of climbers will encourage bushiness too.

Primula malacoides was originally a small wild plant from China, but it has been constantly improved and now has quite large flowers in colours ranging from carmine to dark purple and has become a very popular spring-flowering pot plant. During the autumn and winter they must be kept frost-free, but only need a gentle heat of about 7°C to 10°C. *P. obconica* is also grown as an annual and will, with the minimum of attention, flower for almost the whole year. The flowers form an umbel of up to fifteen large flowers and the colour range takes in shades of red, pink, purple and white. Its large rounded leaves have a rather velvety texture. Contact with some of the hairs, produced chiefly on the stems, sometimes causes an irritating skin rash and susceptible people should wear gloves.

Thunbergia alata (Black-eyed Susan) is a free-flowering climber. It has cream, yellow or orange flowers, with a rich purple throat.

Other annuals which can be raised from seed and potted on are dwarf Antirrhinums, Petunias, Nemesias, Lobelias, and Verbenas. Also *Phlox drummondii* and *Salpiglossis*. Plants such as the Winter Cherry are perennials that can be treated as annuals. Cinerarias may be induced to live for more than one season, but it is not really worth the trouble as it is usually possible to take cuttings.

Begonias

Begonias are usually divided into three groups according to the rooting systems. Tuberous begonias are barely represented among house plants, although popular as greenhouse subjects, but both rhizomatous and fibrous-rooted ones are admirable house plants. Although they have a reputation for difficulty, the majority of house plant begonias will be found easy to cultivate. The one thing they will not tolerate is gas fumes. They like a shady position and to be kept on the dry side, but not too dry, thus they do well if the pot is put into a second, larger pot filled with damp peat.

Leaf patterns of *Begonia rex* and flowers of tuberous begonias *(right)*

Among the most popular of begonias grown for the sake of their leaves are *Begonia rex*. All varieties are rhizomatous and spread outwards, seldom exceeding 10 inches in height, although they may be as much as 12 inches or more across. They have the usual asymmetric triangular leaf and, although variegation in colouring goes through a metallic olive-green, silver grey, dark red and mixtures of these shades, *Begonia rex* are seldom sold as named plants, leaving the customer to choose the one preferred. There is sometimes a flower of rather dirty pinkish white, not decorative, and better removed when it appears. Too low a temperature during winter induces mildew. If it can be detected in time affected leaves should be removed and the plant moved to a warmer situation.

Begonia masoniana is a handsome plant, until recently known as 'Iron Cross' (see page 11). It is hardier than one imagines, not a quick grower and treatment is similar to *B. rex*. *Begonia haageana* used to be seen frequently in cottage windows, and will tolerate more light than many other begonias. It looks at its best with light behind it, as the red underside of the leaves will shine through to great advantage. It soon makes a large plant, but it is necessary to stop it at

Winter-flowering begonia 'Gloire de Lorraine'

regular intervals during the growing season or it will become leggy. The plant is hardy and easy to grow. Flower panicles of pinkish-white are produced in summer.

Begonia 'Abel Carriere' is fibrous rooted, with heart-shaped, glossy leaves, silver coloured with thin dark green zones along the veins. The underside is purple. Stopping should be done early and side shoots should also be stopped to produce a bushy plant. The small red flowers are produced from the leaf axils. Apart from making certain that the leaves are not scorched by sun, it is an easy plant to grow.

*(From left to right) Aechmea
fulgens, Aechmea macracantha
and Tillandsia lindeniana*

Bromeliads

The family Bromeliaceae originated in the American continent
and the Caribbean islands. The family is of purely decorative
interest, although only recently recognized as being particularly suitable for use as house plants. They are surprisingly
hardy plants, capable of surviving low temperatures, and
many of them are extremely spectacular which makes them a
very welcome addition to a list of easily grown house plants.
They are said to withstand frost, but it is wiser not to put this
to the test. The bromeliads cultivated as house plants, are
epiphytes in their native state, growing along the branches of
trees, or occasionally on rocks.

The typical form of most bromeliads is a rosette of leaves
with an empty cup-like space in the centre. This is referred to
as the 'vase' and should be kept full of water, preferably rain
water. Once a bromeliad has flowered the central rosette dies,
leaving a number of off-shoots which will grow best if left
attached to the original plant as long as possible, then potted
on into a mixture of one third leaf mould (oak or birch leaves
if possible), one third *Sphagnum* moss, one third peat. Once

established the plants can be moved into an airy, light position. The best time to take off-shoots is August. They should be placed in the smallest possible pot and only be potted on in absolute necessity. This will be caused by the size of the rosette, not the root action. In the home, bromeliads like as much light as possible.

Aechmea fulgens, a native of Guyana, has dark green, narrow leaves finely spined on the margin and rounded at the ends. The flower is a spike, bearing a panicle of flaming scarlet, and blooms throughout the autumn. They like plenty of light, judicious moderate watering with the central rosette kept full of water, rain water if possible, and leaves wiped free of dust. *A. rhodocyanea*, originally known as *A. fasciata*, produces grey-green rosettes about 12 to 18 inches across. The flower stem bears pink, spiky bracts, which protect pink, blue and violet flowers and which last for a long period. Propagation of all types is by detaching the offsets.

Cryptanthus fosterianus (left)
and *(right) Vriesia splendens*

Ananas comosus is the common Pineapple and it is possible, with care, to grow an attractive house plant that will flower and fruit after a couple of years. A young green Pineapple tuft should be chosen and it should have as little of the fruit flesh on it as possible. It must be potted into moist peat and sand and kept very warm. When a root system is well developed it can be potted into a soil mixture. A flowering plant should be fed freely. Sunlight is essential and cold draughts are lethal. Propagation is by offsets.

Billbergia nutans, an almost hardy native of Brazil, grows with rosettes of narrow, finely spined, grass-like, silvery green leaves, about 12 inches long. The flowers, a drooping spike made up of rose-pink bracts surrounding small greenish-yellow and blue flowers, occur in late winter and early spring. It should be watered freely in summer, less freely in winter and kept at a minimum temperature of 15°C. Propagation is by off-sets in spring.

Cryptanthus fosterianus is a low growing plant that does not have the typical 'vase' of most of the family, which makes watering

Cryptanthus
tricolor

Cryptanthus
acaulis

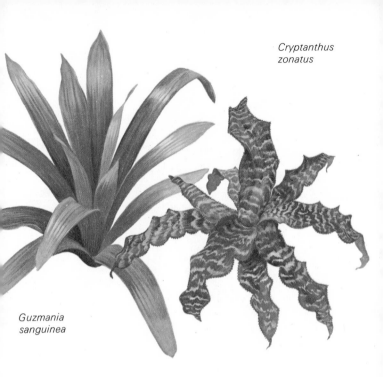

Cryptanthus
zonatus

Guzmania
sanguinea

more difficult. The best method is to keep the compost moist
in summer, dry in winter. Flowers appear in the centre of the
rosette and in the leaf axils, but are not conspicuous. The
leaves are brilliantly coloured with horizontal irregular bands
of red and greyish-white. *C. acaulis*, the Earth Star, is not a
particularly attractive specimen but will look good in arrangements and live almost regardless of attention. The long narrow
leaves of *C. tricolor* are striped with green and cream and have a
pink tinge along the edge. *C. zonatus*, like *C. fosterianus*, is
distinguished by having its colour run across, instead of along,
the length of the leaves. The colour of the bands of *C. zonatus* is
grey. The cryptanthus' are all small-growing and stemless and
C. fosterianus is larger than many. Colour varies with the
intensity of the light.

Guzmania zahnii is a most interesting plant from Costa Rica. The
leaves, with a yellow ground, striped crimson, are about 20
inches long. The upper part of the leaves are also crimson

31

Neoregelia carolinae tricolor

Vriesia
carinata

Nidularium
innocentii

32

while the flower spike consists of a panicle 4 inches across, 9 inches long with a number of yellow flowers that are short-lived, but so numerous that the spike is conspicuous for several weeks. It likes a temperature of 10°C, or over.

Neoregelia carolinae tricolor are like many of the other bromeliads, but the flowers do not appear on a spike, but emerge above the water in the 'vase'. *N. carolinae* has rather narrow leaves of medium green with a centre variegated with cream and pink. The last leaves appear before the flowers are short and very brilliantly coloured; in this species they are bright red. The flowers which appear first from the outside of the flower cluster, are pale blue, about ½ inch across.

Nidularium innocentii is very similar to the last genus making a fair-sized rosette of leaves about 12 inches long, 1½ inches in width. The leaves are very slightly serrated at the edge, dark green, flecked with purple above and a very dark red underneath. As the flowers emerge, the centre of the rosette turns a bright crimson. The flowers, which barely emerge from the water in the 'vase', are greenish-white in colour and of little interest. The plant is quite hardy, but the temperature should not be allowed to drop below 10°C.

Tillandsia lindeniana plants make a rosette, about 20 inches across, of narrow green leaves. The flower shape is very ornamental with pink bracts from which large blue flowers emerge. The bracts keep their colour for about eight weeks, and although the flowers, which start from the bottom of the sheath, only last about four days there is a continual succession and the bracts remain. They require an airy position and bright light and should be kept just moist most of the time.

Vriesia carinata is a small plant with a rosette about 6 inches across with medium green leaves. The keeled bracts (*carinata* means 'keeled') are borne on a stem 4 inches high and are red and yellow, lasting for about eight weeks. The inflorescence is 3 inches long and 2 inches across, with yellow flowers lasting one day. *V. splendens* is often obtainable and has 15 inch long leaves, about 2½ inches wide, with brownish banding. *V. fenestralis* and *V. hieroglyphica* are even bigger plants, the rosettes sometimes being 2 feet across. All species should be given some warmth but they are not susceptible to draughts and will tolerate some sunlight, although shade is preferable.

(From top to bottom) daffodils, crocuses, grape hyacinths and double early tulips

Bulbous and cormous plants

These are grown as temporary house plants and, although they are colourful and much appreciated, they require a rest period after flowering, which is not always possible if one lives in a flat or apartment. Dry, dormant bulbs, for winter or early spring flowering, should be grown in flowerpots in a suitable potting compost. Bowls with no means of drainage should be filled with bulb fibre or pebbles, with a handful of charcoal at the base of the bowl. It is possible to buy prepared bulbs, which have received heat treatment for some weeks before dispatch, and which will start into life more rapidly than unprepared bulbs, but these must be planted when received.

For domestic forcing it is usually convenient to put the pots into a cool, dark cupboard. An average temperature of 10° C is ideal. Once the plants are in their cupboard they need only be inspected once a month to check that soil or fibre is still moist. Once the flower bud has emerged from the bulb the containers can be brought out into a light position, but still kept cool. A warm room will make them grow too fast and the stems will be weak and floppy. When the flower buds are actually visible, the pots and bowls can be brought into a warm room. The above treatment applies to daffodils, narcissus, hyacinths and tulips and the small spring bulbs such as *Crocus, Scilla, Galanthus* (snowdrops) *Chionodoxa* and *Iris reticulata*. Some other bulbs require different treatment. Freesias must be potted up in soil in early autumn with the corms distributed fairly thickly about $\frac{1}{2}$ inch below the surface. The soil should be well watered and the pots placed in a light but shady position. Once the flower buds are formed they can be put in a warmer place.

Amaryllis, correctly *Hippeastrum*, are large bulbs that produce trumpet-shaped flowers, ranging from white to scarlet, during autumn or early spring. They appreciate as much warmth as can be provided and can be grown from dry bulbs or bought already potted up. Once growth has started the *Amaryllis* is treated like any other indoor plant. After flowering the leaves will continue to grow and make a handsome, striking, display.

(From top to bottom) hyacinths, and species of *Lachenalia, Ixia* and *Sparaxis*

The Scarborough Lily, *Vallota purpurea,* is an ideal window plant. Introduced from South Africa in 1774, it owes its common name to its one-time popularity in that town. It has funnel-shaped, bright scarlet flowers in clusters of three to eight at the head of a stout stalk, arising from stiff, upright, broad, linear leaves, about 15 inches long, in early autumn. A little feed, such as liquid manure, will help when buds form. Growth slackens in the spring.

Nerine is native to South Africa and easily grown in pots for the house, to give autumn flowers of great charm. *N. bowdenii* has large umbels of soft pink flowers with recurring petals on 18 inch stalks and there are some other lovely varieties. *N. sarniensis,* the Guernsey Lily, is not quite so large but is glowing salmon in colour, on 2 foot stems, orange-scarlet in the variety *corusca,* and fiery scarlet in the variety *venusta.* All these species flower before the glossy green leaves appear. They must be allowed to die down and be

(From top to bottom) Amaryllis or *Hippeastrum,* freesias, and *Zantedeschia aethiopica*

Lilium auratum (left), nerines *(centre)* and *(right)* the Scarborough Lily, *Vallota purpurea*

kept dry until autumn when watering restarts growth.

Lillies grow well in pots and make good house plants, but they do take up a lot of space. The bulbs are large and must be buried in large pots. *Lilium auratum* has a large head of white trumpet-shaped flowers thickly spotted with golden spots, and with a golden ray down the centre of each petal. *Lilium regale,* with white trumpet-shaped flowers purple-flushed on the outside of the petals, and the small scarlet-flowered *Lilium pumilum* are also suitable, as is the well-known white trumpet lily, *Lilium longiflorum.* The white Arum Lily, *Zantedeschia aethiopica,* does not require a great deal of heat so long as it is not exposed to freezing temperatures, but it does need a fairly large pot. All arums can be given a liquid feed about every ten days when growth is really established and buds are formed. After flowering has finished, when the leaves start to yellow and dry off, watering should be much reduced, but should never be wholly discontinued. If it is possible to put the pots outside during the summer, it will be beneficial. *Ixia, Lachenalia* and *Sparaxis* can also be grown in pots for the house.

Opuntia microdasys (right)
Neoporteria aspillaga (below)

Cacti and succulents

Cacti and succulents are well suited to house culture because
they offer much in the way of interest, are at home in a contemporary setting and yet seem to adapt themselves especially
well if surrounded by Victoriana. They are also welcomed for
their hardiness and toughness under fluctuating indoor
conditions.

Almost all these plants should have maximum sunlight and
dry air and dislike stuffy damp conditions. Too little water
should be given rather than too much, which causes the plants
to rot. Frost is the only major hazard.

Cacti are almost all spiny, with perhaps the exception of
Epiphyllum and *Zygocactus*. They generally take some time
to reach any considerable size. The following selection are
some of the more popular species.

Astrophytum myriostigma is known by the common name of
Bishop's Cap or Bishop's Mitre from the arrangement of the
five deeply divided ribs. Its green appearance is subdued by a
covering of white dots; each a small tuft of white hairs. It
has no spines and will reach 20 inches, although most grow no
larger than 4 or 5 inches. The yellow flowers generally appear

(From left to right) Astrophytum myriostigma, Trichocereus candicans and Mammillaria zielmanniana

freely on plants that are over two or three years old.

Cephalocereus senilis is known as the 'Old Man Cactus' because of the long white hairs that completely cover the plant. Among the hairs grow numerous grey spines. It requires a warm sunny position and frequent watering in summer, taking care not to wet the hairs. It grows slowly.

Lobivia species are globular cacti, sometimes confused with species of *Echinopsis*. The flowers range in colour from deep carmine or bright orange to pale pink or yellow.

Mammillaria zeilmanniana has a glossy green cylindrical body with short hooked spines. It grows freely and the plants will flower when only very small. The flowers are purple with a pale throat and appear at the crown.

Neoporteria species are at first globular and later become more cylindrical in shape. They are generally deeply divided by furrows and have woolly areoles with long spines.

Opuntia microdasys comes from Mexico and is a popular species of cactus. The many-jointed plant can reach a height of 20 inches and the joints can reach 4 inches across. The areoles are yellow, covered with numerous barbed hairs, which can easily penetrate a hand if they are lightly touched. The plant should, therefore, be handled with great care. The yellow flower rarely appears. There is a variety *rufida,* which has red-brown hairs.

Phylocactus hybrids are characterized by having long branches that resemble leaves. In the natural state they are epiphytes and so should be grown in a fibrous soil, shaded from sunlight. The large flowers can be found in a wide range of colours.

Trichocereus candicans can have columnar stems that reach 5 inches after a few years growth. The spines are yellow-gold and brown at the base and make this an attractive plant to grow. It branches from the base and has large, white, lily-like flowers.

Zygocactus truncatus is one of the most popular cacti, especially since it flowers freely during the winter. It is commonly known as the 'Christmas Cactus' or 'Crab Cactus'. The branches are

The long branches of *Phylocactus,* which resemble leaves, with flowers growing from the sides and *Lobivia,* also in flower. *(right)*

segmented and new plants can be started off by placing one or two segments in a suitable growing medium. It is often confused with species of *Epiphyllum* and *Schlumbergera*.

Most succulents are suitable for growing as separate pot plants as they will grow into fairly sizeable specimens quite quickly. They also appear attractive with selections of other plants. Some of those suitable for house cultivation are described as follows.

Agave ferdinandi-regis produces a rosette of very hard leaves, along the edges of which are narrow white lines. At the tip of each leaf are two or three small spines. It does not grow very large and can be kept for a long time in the house. It should have a winter temperature of not less than 10° C.

Aloe variegata (Partridge-breasted Aloe) has dark green, stiff, keeled leaves, banded irregularly across with white markings. This is the show piece of the family and has loose spikes of orange-red flowers in spring. *A. humilis* is a dwarf plant, with very thick, blue-green leaves and white teeth along the edges. There are many varietal forms. *A. mitriformis* grows upright

Zygocactus truncatus,
or Crab Cactus

with a stem and has spoon-shaped leaves edged with pale yellow teeth. The aloes like sun, free watering in summer, little in winter and a temperature above 7°C.

Crassula arborescens will tolerate a wide range of conditions and is very suitable for room culture. To induce the pinkish-white flowers to appear, the plant should be kept cool and dry in a bright situation. There are innumerable species belonging to this genus, all popular and easily cultivated. Two more recently discovered species *C. arta* and *C. columnaris* have a resting period in the summer and should have a winter minimum temperature of at least 10°C.

Cotyledon undulata is widely grown. The leaves are close together on a short stem and have white wavy edges and a waxy coating over the whole leaf. To preserve this covering, plants should be watered from below.

Echeveria species are innumerable and can often be grown outside if they can be wintered under glass. They can be propagated by division, from leaf cuttings or from seed. *Echeveria elegans* has very regular dense rosettes of leaves, each of which has a

Aloe variegata

Lithops

Kalanchoe marmorata

Gasteria verrucosa in flower and *Agave ferdinandi-regis*

distinct point. They are often slightly translucent and reddish around the margins. *E. pulvinata* has the leaves covered with white hairs, which gives it a felt-like appearance. Older leaves turn brownish. The flowers are produced on long leafy stems. ***Gasteria verrucosa*** are invaluable for collections as they will tolerate shade. A minimum temperature of 8°C is adequate for the winter, providing the plants are kept dry. There are many popular species in this genus and this particular plant has 4 to 6 inch long leaves covered with white warts. The upper surface is grooved.

Kalanchoe is a genus of half-hardy succulent plants found chiefly in tropical and South Africa, Madagascar and eastern countries. Their great attraction lies in their attractively coloured leaves and sometimes their bright scented flowers. *K. blossfeldiana* is probably the most successful as a house plant. It is a small shrub about 12 inches high, from Madagascar, producing many stems with dark green notched leaves edged with red, and panicles of small orange-red scented flowers, in the winter months. Two more kalanchoes, *K.*

(From left to right) Sempervivum, the Houseleek, *Echeveria pluvinata* and *Echeveria elegans*

beharensis and *K. tomentosa* are also native to Madagascar. The former has stems up to 2 feet tall and large, heart-shaped, toothed leaves that are rust-red with fine hairs in youth, turning white later. The latter plant is about 18 inches high with thick, small, oval leaves. Silvery hairs give a plush-like feel and are rust-red at the tip. This plant is grown for its foliage as it will not flower.

Kleina articulata (Candle Plant) is a succulent sub-shrub, native to the Canary Islands and South Africa. It grows with erect, round, jointed glaucous-blue stems covered with a grey waxy bloom, which earns it the name Candle Plant. It grows during the winter and produces small leaves, which soon wither, and long-stemmed corymbs of yellowish-white flowers. These plants should be given as much light as possible with a minimum winter temperature of 7°C. Moderate (once a week) watering should be given during the winter and a brief rest after flowering. Propagation is by summer cuttings.

Lithops is a generic name derived from the Greek *'lithos'* meaning 'stone' and *'ops'* meaning 'like'. They are commonly known as 'living stones' and the bodies of the many species

Crassula arborescens (left) and
Cotyledon undulata (above)

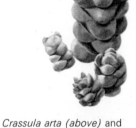

Crassula arta (above) and
Crassula columnaris (below)

may be solitary or in clumps.
Water should be withheld
during winter. The plants
usually make new bodies in
the spring and nutrients are
obtained from the old plants,
which eventually become
skins that are split open by
the developing young leaves.
Sempervivum soboliferum (the
Houseleek) has flattened
rosettes and can usually be
grown outside in a rock
garden. Clumps of plants are
easily separated or single
rosettes detached and rooted.
S. arachnoideum is another
popular species that has stemless rosettes, which have each
leaf terminating in a long,
silky, white hair. This gives
it the appearance of being
covered with a spider's web.

(Above, from left to right) Cobea scandens, *Hoya carnosa,* or Wax Plant and *Passiflora caerula,* or Passion Flower

Climbing plants

These climbing plants are suitable for growing indoors, up central supports in pots, on trellis or as room dividers, and around windows. *Cissus antarctia*, the Kangaroo Vine of Australia, has already been described under hardy house plants (pages 8-9). *Cissus discolor* of Java is much more tender than *C. antarctia*, but is a most beautiful foliage plant for heated rooms providing a winter minimum temperature of 13°C can be maintained. It has long, heart-shaped and pointed, velvety-green leaves, marbled white between the veins and with purple and crimson tinting.

Cobea scandens from tropical America, is an ornamental climber of such rapid growth that it can come into flower, from seed, in a very few months. It climbs by tendrils with pinnate leaves, made up of oval leaflets, and its flowers are carried on single stems, about 6 inches long. The flowers themselves, large and bell-shaped, are pale green at first, changing with age to violet-blue. Pot culture helps control its growth, but judicious pruning may be needed during the early stages. During summer it needs frequent watering and light, airy conditions. In winter the plant can be rested until early spring in a minimum temperature of 7° to 10°C, then pruned severely and the soil top-dressed. Propagation is by seed or it can be treated as an annual and replaced each year, thus avoiding housing it during the dormant period.

Ficus radicans variegata is a small-leaved creeping, or climbing, fig with leaves up to $2\frac{1}{2}$ inches long, an inch across and tapering to a point, with the leaf edged slightly waved. It is difficult to keep and needs a warm and moist atmosphere. The thin branches, which will trail or climb, are thickly covered with the cream or green leaves and side shoots are produced naturally, although stopping will encourage them.

Hoya carnosa has thick, glossy leaves, about $1\frac{1}{2}$ to 3 inches in length. It will tolerate cool conditions and flower in warmer ones. The plants climb easily and have aerial roots. The variety *variegata* is often grown for its foliage, and rarely flowers. *Passiflora caerulea* is a half hardy climber often grown for its profuse foliage. It is usually known as the Passion Flower and has been given this name because it is said to bear, in its curiously formed flowers, the instruments of the Crucifixion.

47

Coloured foliage plants

The foliage of many of the house plants grown today is of such outstanding beauty and has the most exquisite markings, colouring and shape of leaf, that one is tempted to grow nothing but coloured foliage pot plants. Alas, they need a great deal of light to retain those perfect shades, so perhaps it is as well that one can, as a rule, find space for only a few.

Acalypha wilkesiana marginata, which came from Fiji nearly a century ago and is obtainable as a house plant from specialist suppliers, needs a humid atmosphere, like all the members of the spurge family. It has large, slightly coarse, leaves of olive green, with broad margins of carmine, which much appreciate being syringed with tepid water in summer.

Acalypha wilkesiana marginata

Caladium have the most spectacular shaped and coloured leaves, from green with white or pink markings, to all-red. The length of the leaf varies from 6 inches to 3 feet. The plants require plenty of warmth and water while the leaves are growing.

Coleus originated in the tropics of the Old World and, although there are over 100 species, only one of the species, *C. blumei,* a perennial from Java, is cultivated as a house plant. About 12 to 18 inches tall, with broad-based, ovate, coarsely-toothed leaves, which grow in opposite pairs up the stems, it is rather similar to a nettle, but there the resemblance ends, for *C. blumei* has leaves that are beautifully coloured and variegated. As ornamental foliage plants in a diversity of contrasting colours, crimson, maroon, yellow, bronze, brown, green and white they make magnificent pot plants. Plants may be bought in named varieties, such as 'Verschaffiltii', 'Golden Ball', 'Princess Elizabeth' and 'Sunset', or more simply grown from selected strains of seed, which will yield plants in a wide variety and combination of colours. They will do well, given good light and airy conditions, in warm rooms with regular watering

Some varieties of *Coleus*

when in active growth. Flower shoots, uninteresting and inconspicuous, should be pinched out in the interest of leaf growth. If the plants are to be kept from one year to the next, they will need a winter temperature of 13°C, very moderate watering and no draughts. Propagation is by seed in spring, or by young cuttings of favourite plants at any time.

Cordyline terminalis can, in theory, reach a height of 5 to 12 feet, but in practice rarely exceeds 18 inches. The original plant from New Zealand has plain green leaves, but the numerous varieties contain some brilliant colours. The leaves may be as much as 12 inches long and 4 inches across, shaped in

49

an elongated oval. The plants are rather expensive to buy, as the young plants do not show the brilliant colours and have to be grown on in the nursery for some years before they can be offered for sale. They should be given plenty of water and as much humidity and warmth as possible, but not direct sunlight. Propagation is by cuttings.

Dieffenbachia amoena has shining green leaves covered with cream and white blotches. All species are highly poisonous but will grow well in most conditions, providing a temperature of $12°C$ can be maintained (see page 15).

Gynura scandens, possibly known as *Gynura sarmentosa*, is an attractive, rapidly-growing plant with slate-blue leaves tinged with red or purple. It should have as much light as possible, but kept out of scorching sun. Shade will make it produce thin, drawn shoots, but pinching out will produce a bushy plant. If it is not pinched out it will grow at an alarming rate, producing very small leaves. It should be kept rather dry in winter, as wet soil and low temperatures may result in rotting. It needs plenty of water in summer.

Pelargonium zonale is rather a grand sounding, but strictly accurate, name for the ordinary geranium, one of the finest house plants. In a sunny window it will continue flowering for months, with the minimum of attention. They are not difficult house plants, but they must have maximum light. There are numerous variegated leaved varieties, of which 'Henry Cox' is a brilliant example, with its leaves of cream, green, scarlet and black. 'Happy Thought', with leaves of green, marked on each leaf with a lemon coloured butterfly shape is also most attractive.

Rhoeo discolor (Boat Lily) is an unusual, attractive, not too easily grown house plant that is rather fussy about the treatment it receives. It has long, narrow, fleshy leaves growing out horizontally from a central stem, which are olive green above and bright purple underneath. It has tiny white or blue flowers, formed at the base of the stem, growing in curious boat-shaped, purple bracts, which has inspired its common name of Boat Lily. This plant comes from Central America and needs partial shade, good ventilation and fairly liberal watering from spring to autumn, very moderate watering in winter and a winter minimum temperature of $10°C$.

Diffenbachia amoena

Rhoeo discolor

Cordyline terminalis

51

Cyclamen 'Rose of Zehlendorf' *(above)* and 'Rhodese' *(right)*

Cyclamen

Cyclamen are not easy to grow. If rooms are kept at a temperature of 21°C during the winter, no attempt should be made to grow them. A cyclamen received as a flowering plant from the florist will have been grown in a humid greenhouse where it enjoyed a night temperature maintained at around 10°C, rising to around 15°C during the day. If it can be given approximately these conditions in the home, all may be well. It will not be possible to match them exactly, but a cool room with an east window in which the plant can stand, or a slightly heated enclosed porch with plenty of light, yet shaded from bright light except in the early morning, are very suitable. The soil should never be allowed to become dry during the time the plant is in bloom; nor at any time should water touch the corm, which is set half-in and half-out of the soil in the pot.

The cyclamen is one of the most popular winter-flowering pot plants in Europe, but not in the United States where the rooms are normally kept at too high a temperature, with too dry an atmosphere, for the cyclamen to survive. The peak period of demand for cyclamen is at Christmas, which is the most difficult time for trying to keep them in the house.

Success is more likely with the earlier flowering plants obtainable from July onwards, or the later flowering ones obtainable in March. It is quite possible to have success with them at Christmas but the leaves are more prone to go yellow and the very young buds sometimes fail to mature.

Cyclamen dislike temperatures that fluctuate widely. A room that is hot and dry in the afternoon and evening and cools down rapidly at night, is almost exactly the opposite of what they need, which is an even temperature not above 15°C, fresh air, and a slightly moist atmosphere. They dislike draughts, and a well-lit hall or bedroom will probably be a more congenial situation than a living room. The roots are not particularly active at this time, and too wet a soil can be disastrous, with leaves yellowing and unopened buds rotting off. The soil should never be more than moist, which in practice means fairly frequent watering but with very small

A white cyclamen provides attractive relief in this bowl of foliage plants

Cyclamen persicum 'White Swan'

Cyclamen persicum,
silver leaf variety
(right) and a strain of
*Cyclamen persicum
giganteum (below)*

quantities of water at a time. The atmosphere around the plant can be improved by spraying the leaves daily with a very fine spray, but water should not be allowed to get on to the flowers. There are two ways of watering the plant depending on whether the corm is above the surface of the soil, or whether the corm is buried. If it is above the surface soil, it can be watered from the top avoiding the corm; if buried, it is better to hold the pot for a minute in water that does not come over the rim. During frosty weather the plants should be moved from a position near the window at night and placed in the centre of the room.

There is no need to feed a fully mature cyclamen but it is helpful to the plant to put the pot in a larger bowl filled with moist peat or moss. The top of the pot should project slightly above the level of the moss or peat, and the moist atmosphere that this provides will do more good than water at the roots. The modern silver leaf strain not only has most ornamental leaves, but stands up better to home conditions than many other strains. The foliage is compact, on short stems and the flowers are on sturdy stems that do not flop.

C. persicum is the cyclamen from which most greenhouse and commercial cyclamen have been derived. Native to eastern Mediterranean countries, several strains have been bred and there are many named varieties such as 'Afterglow' which is scarlet, 'Crimson King' crimson, 'Rosalie' light salmon-rose, 'White Swan' white, 'Salmon King' salmon pink, 'Rose von Aalsmeer' rose pink and 'Grandiflora' white with crimson base. A root will flower for several years, with more flowers but which tend to be smaller in size. When the plants have finished flowering, they should be moved to a greenhouse or frame, from which frost can be excluded. They must be given as much air and light as possible and not allowed to suffer from lack of moisture. The old idea of drying off the corm has been found to be a fallacy. During the summer, if possible, it is best to bury them in a shady part of a garden and leave them there. By late summer they will have lost all their foliage. The top 2 inches of soil must then be removed and replaced with an equal amount of potting compost. They should be well watered and stood in a shady frame. By autumn they will have good healthy leaves, and can be grown on as usual.

Ferns

Many plants in the foliage classification are, technically, flowering plants, although their flowers may have little ornamental value. Even *Aspidistra*, a foliage plant if ever there was one, has purple-maroon flowers an inch across, yet many people grow it for years, never seeing the annual flowers, so shyly are they displayed. Ferns are, however, definitely flowerless plants making up for this by the elegance and beauty of their fronds. Many ferns naturally inhabit shaded places and are able to thrive in a subdued light, which makes them particularly useful in dimly lighted locations in the house.

Adiantum pedatum is the popular and beautiful 'Maidenhair Fern'. The finely divided leaves are from 4 to 16 inches wide and almost horseshoe-shaped. The leaf stalk is wiry and a shiny black. *Adiantum* grows easily does not need much heat but does need humidity, in common with most ferns. Propagation is by root division in the spring.

Asparagus plumosus is so well-known as the 'Asparagus Fern' that it is included here. It is, however, not a fern at all but a berry-bearing evergreen climber. The leaves are various colours of green, feathery, and may be trained up wires or

Adiantum the 'Maidenhair Fern' *(left)* and *Platycerium* the 'Stag's Horn Fern' *(below)*

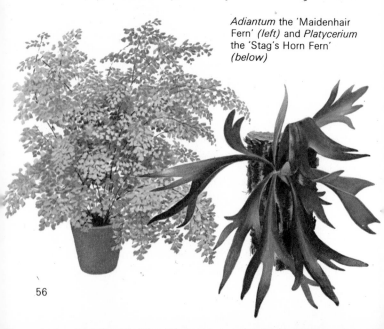

strings. It welcomes good light, free watering and syringing in the summer, very moderate watering in winter and a minimum winter temperature of 10° to 13°C. *Asparagus sprengeri* is an emerald green climber, good for hanging baskets, with needle-like leaves and small white flowers on the adult plant followed by red berries. A humidity lover, this plant should be sprayed frequently and given plenty of water when growing. It is best grown in partial shade and should be kept out of the sun, which might discolour the foliage. A winter temperature of 12°C should be maintained. All *Asparagus* need feeding for most of the year and plants should have monthly doses of a liquid manure when fully established.

Asplenium nidis (Bird's Nest Fern) is striking for its bright green undivided fronds, springing 2 to 4 feet in length and which make a nest formation at the crown. It has a variety, *australiasicum*, in which the midribs of the leaves are black. This plant requires moist, heated, conditions, a minimum winter

Asparagus sprengeri (top)
Asparagus plumosus (right)

Asplenium nidus

Nephrolepis exaltata,
Boston Fern

temperature of 15°C and shade. It should be watered liberally in summer, more moderately in winter.

Nephrolepis exaltata (Boston Fern) is one of the tropical ferns that can be used in the house. It has finely cut, pinnate fronds of up to 2 feet long, 6 inches broad, growing rapidly and, therefore, requiring a fair amount of space. There are several more beautiful species such as *N. magnifica* and *N. whitmanii*, in which the fronds are more finely cut. *N. cordifolia compacta* is another useful plant of a deep glossy green colour, with arching fronds, again about 2 feet long. These ferns like a summer temperature of about 21°C, with shade and liberal watering and winter temperature of a minimum of 10°C and more moderate watering.

Phoenix dactylifera (Phoenix Palm) is the Date Palm of North Africa and Arabia and is an attractive pot plant with grey-green leafleted leaves that arch gracefully. It will grow well indoors for a number of years. The plant needs copious watering throughout the summer, with frequent sponging of the foliage if it is kept in warm rooms. Only moderate watering and a minimum temperature of 13°C is necessary to maintain it in winter.

Phyllitis scolopendrium (Hart's Tongue Fern) is hardy and makes a decorative pot plant for cool or unheated rooms. The bright green strap-like leaves are 6 to 12 inches long and especially attractive are the more sophisticated varieties such as *crispum,* which has frilled edges, and *cristatum* with its crested fronds. The species are very variable, so it is as well to choose your plants at the nurseries. Virtually evergreen, these plants like shady quarters and regular watering in summer, rather less in winter with a minimum temperature of 7°C. Propagation is by division in spring.

Platycerium bifurcatum, often known as *P. alicorne,* is commonly called the 'Stag's Horn Fern' (see page 17).

Pteris cretica has fronds that reach 1 foot in length and comes from tropical areas. There are numerous varieties. It should be grown in a peaty compost and positioned in a shady part of the room. It can be watered freely in summer moderately during the winter months and the temperature should never be allowed to fall below 10°C.

Phyllitis scolopendrium

Pteris cretica

Ficus (Figs)

These house plants are one of the most rewarding of all the genera. They are easy to keep, tolerant of low temperatures and in a surprisingly short time make handsome plants which, if looked after well, continue to be handsome practically indefinitely. It is advisable to let new growth emerge under shady conditions so the leaves will expand more fully. They do not like to be in continuous draught and the plants have a decided rest period when they should be kept on the dry side, but not allowed to dry out completely. Growth restarts in late spring, when water should be given more regularly, though never overdone. Overwatering causes the leaves to turn yellow or go brown at the edges and, since the leaves are usually thick and leathery, this means that damage has been done before any symptoms were noticed. Once damage has started it will continue for some time even if watering is stopped immediately. Watering, but not overwatering, should be recommenced after about a week. Excessive drought, on the other hand, will cause the lower leaves to drop off so great care must be taken with its application, especially in winter. If a thorough watering is given when necessary and then no more until the pot has dried out, no difficulties should be experienced. *Ficus* are quite tolerant of varying temperatures but grow best in a steady temperature of about 12°C. If additional feeding is necessary, one of the compound manures is suitable. *Ficus* do not like over-potting and are quite happy in a pot that looks far too small for the plant. A 5 inch pot will hold a 3 feet high *Ficus* quite happily.

Ficus benjamina an Indian fig does not look like a *Ficus* at all. It has long thin leaves, which are ovate, and leathery, up to 4 inches long and $1\frac{1}{2}$ inches across, forming a graceful weeping plant. Because of the nature of its growth it is often known as the 'Weeping Fig'; from the central stem, which usually needs some support, drooping branches fall, carrying the leaves. The culture of this species is similar to that of the upright growing species, although for the climbers a minimum of 13°C is preferable.

Ficus elastica decora (India-rubber plant) has dark green leathery leaves with a prominent midrib, which is red on the underneath on the youngest leaves (see page 9). The leaves are oblong and

Ficus benjamina (right) and *(below)*
Ficus elastica decora tricolor. (Bottom)
Ficus pumila

61

Ficus lyrata, the 'Fiddle-leaf Fig'

lanced-shaped 9 to 12 inches long and 5 to 7 inches wide. They grow spirally up the stem, attached by slender stalks about an inch long. At the top of the stem is a bright red sheath looking rather like a spike, covering the next leaf to emerge. When the leaf does emerge the coloured sheath falls back and falls off. The central stem will need support for the first few years but as the plant strengthens and ages it will grow straight up naturally without any further trouble. Large leaves often get dusty and should be wiped regularly with a soft cloth and water only. Propagation is by leaf cuttings or air layering.

Ficus elastica doescheri has longer and narrower leaves than *decora.* They emerge as a light green tinged with pink and with a wide cream margin. The petioles and midribs of the younger leaves are pale pink on both sides but this is only temporary, after a year they will both have turned green. As further new leaves emerge, the plant gains in interest. Like many variegated plants it appreciates a warmer position than *F. e. decora.*

Ficus lyrata, known also as *F.*

pandurata, is slightly more difficult to grow. The leaves are 'waisted' so that they appear fiddle-shaped and the plant is commonly known as the 'Fiddle-leaf Fig'. They are likely to fall if the temperature fluctuates too much and require good warmth during the winter. The leaves may also fall if the plant is watered with too cold water, or chlorinated water, and tepid rainwater is the ideal medium.

Ficus pumila is a climber, native to China and Japan, totally dissimilar from the tree species. Its thin stems are heavily dressed in a foliage of small, heart-shaped leaves about an inch long, and fine branches that creep, and being equipped with aerial roots like ivy, can cling or climb. Relatively hardy, and welcoming shade, it is an excellent climbing plant for the house.

Ficus radicans is another creeper, from the East Indies, with 2 inch broad lance-shaped and pointed leaves. It is particularly attractive in the cream and green variety *variegata*. It can be grown as a trailing plant or climber with support, but needs to be given warm and moist conditions.

Ficus radicans variegata

Flowering pot plants

Various flowering pot plants are commonly grown for sale by nurseries and shops. They are very delightful to have in the house, although they do not always adjust immediately to their new surroundings. A close look at their particular requirements will usually explain the reason why.

Aechmea rhodocyanea is probably the most popular of the flowering bromeliad family and is best purchased when in bud. The broad, recurving leaves, spreading 2 feet or more across, form a pale silvery-grey rosette. The upright flower spike is covered with rose-pink bracts. Small flowers of pink and blue open in the axils of the bracts and are produced over a long period, the inflorescence remains colourful for about four months. *A. rhodocyanea* requires an even temperature, just above 7°C, and light shade. Once the flower is over, the main plant will gradually die, but it will have formed two or three off-shoots round its base, the 'vases' of which must be kept filled with water. In late spring they may be removed and potted up in as small a pot as possible.

Anthurium has some 500 species belonging to the genus but only one seems suitable for house conditions. Known as *Anthurium scherzerianum* it was introduced from Costa Rica

Aechmea rhodocyanea

in 1880 and is a member of the Arum family. It has attractive long, leathery, dark green leaves, pointed at the tip, rounded at the base and borne on wiry stems about 6 inches high. The striking flowers consist of a brilliant scarlet open oval spathe, with an orange-coloured spadix rising above, like a pig's curly tail, on a long stalk. Many other coloured forms have since been developed. It needs ample light, even temperatures with winter minimum of a steady 15°C and freedom from draught. It also requires a moist atmosphere and will enjoy having its pot put into a second outer pot containing moist peat or moss.

Astilbe japonica gives large panicles of white blooms on slender stems growing out of a bed of fern-like foliage. They should be brought into a cool room in winter and moved into a warmer room, about 13°C, some three weeks later placing them in a sunny position and increasing watering. After flowering, they may be planted outdoors. Propagation is by division the following spring.

Billbergia nutans is another popular bromeliad, which will produce its flowers in a warm room while many others of the family will not. The rosette reaches 1 foot and the dark green leaves are narrow and spiny. The flowers are tubular and various colours, but the plant must be pot-bound to flower.

Anthurium (right)
and *Astilbe (below)*

Bougainvillea glabra

Bougainvillea gives a most exotic effect indoors and *B. glabra,* the easiest one to grow, will flower when only a foot high. It will continue to grow to reach 6 or even 10 feet in height. The inflorescence consists of comparatively insignificant tubular flowers surrounded by showy, rose-coloured bracts throughout the summer. They will tolerate quite low temperatures during their dormant period and during spring and summer they should be kept in a warm room, 15°C, and given as much light as possible. They rarely exceed 18 inches in height the first year and can be pruned back each spring. If they have to live in the house all the time, the growth of the plants and their flowering period will be delayed.

Campanula is a large genus that contains some 300 species yet only two or three can adapt themselves to growing in the house. One of these is *C. isophylla,* a dainty prostrate growing, small leaved perennial. The trailing stems are covered with salver-shaped lilac-blue flowers in midsummer. There is a white flowering form, *C. alba* and another, *C. mazi,* which is also white, but with variegated woolly leaves. This latter is now rather rare but *C. isophylla* is quite easily purchased in a pot. They are herbaceous plants and must be kept dry and frost-free during the dormant winter period. In early spring they can be watered and brought into a warmer position to start them into fresh growth. They should be grown under light, airy conditions, watered and fed freely in growth.

Columnea are epiphytic and are members of the same family as the saintpaulias. They are native to tropical America and make attractive house plants, especially if they can be accommodated in hanging baskets where their trailing stems can drape and show off the brilliantly coloured flowers. Columneas should be kept in a light position and on the dry side when not in flower. They like a minimum temperature of 15°C in winter and a daily spray of tepid water. They flower in autumn and winter and if they are still given this tepid spray after the flowers have faded, they should appear again a month or so later. After four flowerings it is wise to let the plant make some growth which can be used as cuttings in summer.

Columnea gloriosa purpurea (above), Billbergia nutans (below)

Campanula isophylla

Gloxinia

Erica nivalis and *Erica gracilis* are winter-flowering Cape heaths from South Africa. *E. gracilis* makes a bushy plant of 12 to 18 inches, with tiny leaves in fours along its erect stems, and terminal flower clusters of egg-shaped deep pink bells on small side shoots. *E. nivalis* bears white flowers, but the most popular species is *E. hyemalis,* which has upright stems carrying tapering racemes of long, tubular, white, rose-tinted, drooping flowers. All heaths welcome light airy conditions but these plants are difficult to keep alive, especially when first purchased. They are usually sold in small pots and, if they are allowed to become very dry, they will probably not recover. There are two ways to deal with this. The first method is to pot the heather into a larger pot the moment it is received. The newly potted heath should then be well-watered and not allowed to get dry, but it is also necessary to guard against excessive wetness, until roots have penetrated the new soil. The other method is to place the pot in a container keeping $\frac{1}{2}$ inch of water permanently in this second container, while regularly watering the plant from the top. The residue of water in the outer container will prevent any fatal drying-out and the plant can be potted-on after it has flowered. This latter is a fairly safe treatment in centrally heated rooms, but in rooms where the temperature drops at night, there is a risk of root-rot. Once flowering has finished the plants should be kept in fairly cool conditions and a well lit position.

Gloxinia is a member of the same family as *Columnea*, but is native to Brazil. They are notable for their large flowers, which are similar in shape to those of a foxglove but velvety-textured, and the rather rough-textured, heart-shaped, pointed, toothed leaves. These popular house plants are really hybrids from *Sinningia speciosa*. Exceptional strains of these decorative flowering plants have been raised, with flowers borne more erectly and flaring wider at the mouth and with a colour range from pure white to deep crimson. Specialist growers' lists should be consulted for named forms. Plants flower throughout the summer and appreciate a moist atmosphere without direct sunlight. After flowering water should be withheld and the plants will gradually die down. The tubers will over-winter at a temperature of about 10°C. They should be repotted in spring and given a temperature of 18°C. Once rooted, a moderate amount of feeding may be given.

South African heaths;
Erica nivalis (left) and
Erica hyemalis (below)

Flowering shrubs

The following selection are some of the most attractive flowering shrubs for the house.

Abutilon belong to the Mallow family. Several of the shrubby or semi-climbing plants of this genus make ornamental house plants. The evergreen Brazilian *A. megapotamicum* makes a graceful plant with heart-shaped slender-pointed leaves and flowers produced freely from the leaf axils. These are bell-like with a red calyx, yellow petals, and a head of purple-brown stamens and pistils, which grows to about 3 feet. *A. striatum thompsonii* has mottled green and yellow leaves with orange flowers, opening in early summer. It is easily culti-vated where temperatures in winter of $7°$ to $13°$C, and in summer $15°$ to $18°$C can be provided. Plenty of water should be given during the growing season and these plants like mild applications of liquid fertilizer during the flowering season.

Azalea indica (Indian Azalea) is a very popular winter-flower-ing plant, usually purchased when in flower and will remain so for many weeks, if looked after properly. They can be obtained in shades of pink, scarlet, maroon, purple and white. It is best to buy plants that are mainly in bud, one or two

Azalea indica, Indian Azalea

Abutilon 'Master Hugh' *(above)*
and *Abutilon megapotamicum (right)*

showing the colour to ensure that one is getting the shade preferred. This will give more flowering time and less risk of damage during transit. It will not need feeding when in bud or flower. Rain water should be used, if possible, for watering, preferably at room temperature. Azaleas do not like cold water out of the tap. An occasional bucket-bath is appreciated, immersing the plant in a bucket of water and removing it only when the air bubbles stop rising. Normally the buds or flowers show their need for water by wilting slightly. When flowering is over, all dead flowers should be removed, the branches lightly pruned, the plants kept in a warm position and, although less water is required, they must not be allowed to dry out. The plant can be allowed to harden and when all risk of frost is past they can be put outside in a moderately shady position. They should then be watered moderately and will benefit from some fertilizer. Before there is any risk of frost they should be brought back into the house, placed in a well-lit position, feeding stopped and only a moderate amount of water given until buds begin swelling. More water will be required now and heat can be increased to 12° to 15°C.

Euphorbia splendens, Crown of Thorns *(left),* Genista *(right)*

Citrus mitis (Calamondin) is a miniature orange tree which fruits earlier in life than *C. sinensis,* for example, which takes a long time to mature. The calamine orange fruits are edible but rather sharp tasting. Light and air are essential for growth and a minimum winter temperature of 10°C should be arranged. When it is in flower it will need a moist atmosphere which will keep the flowers and set the fruit. Plants are at their best in winter and during the summer the pots can stand outside in the sunniest position available.

Cytisus canariensis is popularly known as Genista. A free branching shrub, it bears its bright yellow, pea-like flowers in short racemes on young shoots in spring. They like a moderate temperature, about 12°C, plenty of light and moderate watering. After flowering it should be pruned lightly and, when all risk of frost is over, it can be put outside in the sunniest possible situation. It should not be allowed to dry out and should be fed every three weeks with a liquid fertilizer. It must be brought under cover before autumn frosts.

Euphorbia pulcherrima is the botanical name for the Poinsettia which was discovered in Mexico in the late 1820s by a Dr

Euphorbia pulcherrima,
Poinsettia

Citrus mitis

Poinsett. In its wild state it grows as a large shrub, and this made it difficult for growers to produce a conveniently sized pot plant. Chemicals for dwarfing the plants are only available to commercial growers at present, so poinsettias must be bought already in flower from florists or nurseries. They have a vigorous root system and thrive well in a temperature between 15°C and 18°C, although a temperature of 10°C is sufficient if necessary. The plants will not require much water. A bought plant will have been well fed, and will need no further feeding during its flowering period. When flowering has finished the head must be cut off and watering stopped. In spring the plant should be put in a warm position, given a good watering and then cut back, leaving about 4 inches of stem, and allowed to start into growth. When growths are about 3 inches long the plants can be potted up into small pots and put in a well-lit position in a warm place. When the new roots appear round the edge of the soil ball and the shoots elongate, plants can be put into larger pots and should be kept at a

73

temperature of 15°C. Many other related species are also popular as house plants. *E. splendens* is commonly known as the 'Crown of Thorns' for it has prickly spines and tiny scarlet flowers like drops of blood. It is a semi-succulent and requires little water, especially in winter. Regular feeding in summer will encourage flower growth.

Hydrangea is one of the most popular flowering shrubs grown for the house. Although there are a large number of hydrangeas in general cultivation the species that is grown as a flowering pot plant is *H. macrophylla*. Normally forced in a 5-inch pot they are ready for sale in late spring and have about a five month flowering period as a pot plant. The 'Lace Cap' varieties are becoming very popular and are being grown in increasing numbers each year. When hydrangeas are bought in flower they should be placed in a very well lit position, but not in direct sun. They need a lot of water, regular feeding and should not be allowed to dry out. They can be stood in a small quantity of water, but not deeper than $\frac{1}{8}$ inch. They do not require great heat at any time. Plants from shops have

Red Garnette Rose *(above)* and *Passiflora caerulea*, Passion Flower, *(below)*

74

often been forced too much and ought to be discarded after flowering, unless you have a garden where they can be planted in a westerly or south-westerly aspect.

Jasminum polyanthum, from China, is a vigorous climber, with pinkish-white, sweet smelling flowers. It is often bought as a pot plant already in bud, with a supporting wire hoop inserted in the pot, around which the growing shoot is twined. As the plant is a vigorous grower it will twine around the hoop many times. It will grow best with full exposure to sun. It should not be fed and little watering is required, but it must not be allowed to dry out completely. If possible, it should be stood outside in the summer.

Passiflora caerulea, a native of South America, is used extensively throughout Europe for indoor decoration, either as a trailing or climbing plant. It has white, green and blue flowers. It should be planted in a large pot and given a position in light airy conditions and supports up which it can climb. Water must be given liberally in the warm months and it should be sprayed frequently. Plants should be kept fairly dry in winter, temperature at a minimum of 10°C, and flowered shoots must be cut away to within two basal buds.

Plumbago capensis is a lovely climbing South African shrub that, grown as a house plant, reaches 3 to 6 feet high and needs

Hydrangea macrophylla (left) and a 'Lace Cap' variety *(below)*

Jasminum polyanthum

some support for its tendrils. The pale blue spikes of flowers, with long corollas, are produced freely in summer. It likes a light airy position and to be watered freely in summer, decreasing gradually thereafter. When it has finished flowering, the flowered shoots should be pruned back to within an inch of their base, as flowers will be produced on new shoots of the current year's growth. The plant needs a summer temperature of 13° to 18°C. A winter temperature of 7°C is essential, preferably in a cool greenhouse or plant room, and it should be given just sufficient water to keep it from drying out. Propagation is by cuttings of side shoots in spring or summer.

Rosa 'Red Garnette' is now becoming popular as a flowering pot plant. Originally patented in the United States after it had been discovered in Germany, it was not very popular when it appeared on the English market, although it was much sought in the United States. It is now, however, very popular in many areas. The red variety is known as Red Garnette. Other varieties are 'Carol' (pink), sometimes known as Pink Garnette, and a yellow one.

Red Garnette has small flowers, which are double and slightly fragrant, and healthy dark green foliage. It grows about 18 inches high and usually has one strong shoot with a truss of flowers, surrounded by smaller shoots with fewer flowers. The foliage being tough and a good dark green makes an excellent setting for the flowers and the general effect is of a bushy compact plant. It grows best in a light situation and should be kept rather moist. When the plant has finished flowering it can be lightly pruned and planted outside in the garden, where it will do well, provided heavy pruning is avoided. Indoor temperature should be about 13°C.

Stephanotis floribunda, a native of Madagascar, is very similar to *Jasminum polyanthum* but the flowers are more waxy and the plants need much more heat. If at all possible they should be given a temperature of about 21°C in spring and summer and a minimum of 12°C during the winter. There should be plenty of watering in the summer and moderate watering in winter. The shoots must be cut back after flowering to keep the plant compact.

Stephanotis floribunda

Fuchsias

In the years before 1914 *Fuchsia* hybrids were some of the most popular pot plants. When, after the Second World War, the interest in pot plants was revived, different types of plants were introduced and the fuchsias were overlooked in favour of foliage plants that were better suited to modern decor and design. That they play an important part in contemporary decor is not to be denied, but there is still a part to be played by the flowering foliage plant.

The first thought when growing indoors should be the choice of variety. Variety is important if only for the fact that some fuchsias will retain their buds and flowers even in the driest conditions while others will immediately drop every flower and bud at the first suggestion that they should move indoors. Some people, not wishing to send to a nursery for two or three plants, may make a choice from a local market stall or chain store. It is worth noting that the vast majority of fuchsias offered for sale in this way are the varieties kept alive from that era when every other house had its fuchsia plant. Varieties such as 'Fascination', 'Ballet Girl', 'Mrs. Marshall', and 'Achievement' have lived for many years as

Fuchsia 'Display'

78

room plants. They have proved that they can hold on tenaciously to life and are therefore quite a sound buy. Some other fuchsias that are suitable for the house are described in the following paragraphs or illustrated on these pages.

'Display' has single flowers. The tube and sepals are rose-pink, the corolla deeper pink. The plant holds its flowers remarkably well under house conditions. These are a distinctive shape, having a saucer-shaped corolla and are borne in great numbers.

'Petite' is a double variety. A very heavy blooming plant, it has small flowers on an upright bushy shrub. The tube and sepals are pale rose and the corolla lilac-blue, fading to a lavender-blue. It flowers early in the season and maintains a profusion of blooms on the plant throughout the summer.

'Pink Jade' has single flowers. The tube and sepals are pink, shading to green at the tips, the corolla orchid pink with a picotee edge of rose. The corolla is saucer-

(From top to bottom) Fuchsia fulgens, 'White Queen' and 'Tennessee Waltz'

79

shaped in much the same manner as 'Display'. The shrub is short-jointed and slow-growing but produces its flowers quite freely.

'Scabieuse' has double, medium-sized flowers that have a red tube and sepals. The corolla is made up of outer petals, which are white suffused with blue, and the inner purple petals. It holds its flowers well.

'William Silver' is another double variety with a red tube and sepals and the corolla is red with definite pink stripes in it. It is extremely free-flowering and produces its flowers over a long period.

A weak feed once a fortnight is sufficient to sustain a fuchsia through its growing season. Growth benefits greatly if the top and undersides of the leaves are sprayed daily. This regular spraying will also deter attacks by insect pests. From early autumn, even if it is still blooming strongly, the plant should be gradually brought to rest. Little by little, water should be withheld from the plant. It should not be allowed to become dust-dry, but eventually only enough water should be given to keep the compost very slightly moist. If it is possible for

'Falling Stars'

'Emile de Wildman'

the fuchsia to spend a few weeks outside at this time, it will allow the existing wood to ripen.

It is necessary to bring the plant indoors when frost threatens and put it in a greenhouse, frost-proof garage, shed or cellar. The plant must not be forgotten but looked at once a fortnight to see that the compost has not dried out or that the plant is not breaking into premature growth. If the compost is found to be very dry it should be thoroughly moistened by placing the whole plant in a bucket of tepid water until bubbles cease rising to the surface. This should last the plant for several weeks. If the plant is seen to be breaking into premature growth it means that the storage conditions are far too warm and it must be moved to a cooler place. When brought out of winter storage in late spring the fuchsia should be placed in a light airy place and, when growth starts, it should be re-potted into a fresh clean pot. As much as possible of the old soil and dead root should be removed and replaced with fresh compost. When growth is again under way, the fuchsia should be pruned. It is better to prune the branches down to the lowest active growth.

Hedera canariensis foliis variegatis

Hedera helix
'Chicago'

Hedera helix
sagittaefolia

Hedera helix
'Little
Diamond'

Ivies

Most of the ivies have proved themselves extremely useful as house plants. They are, on the whole, very hardy. They will put up with considerable neglect, are tolerant of gas fumes, will grow in any soil and do not need frequent repotting. They produce aerial roots both as a form of support and a means of nourishment, their cost is low and they are very easily propagated. Ivies need moist cool conditions during the summer and a weekly spray. Spraying them on both sides of the leaves will prevent attacks by spider mites and scale insects, their worst enemies.

The majority of ivies are cultivars of *Hedera helix,* the common wild ivy and some of them have been given Latin varietal names. The various forms of *Hedera helix* are small-leaved, while *Hedera canariensis,* the Canary Island Ivy, produces large leaves. *Helix* is the Latin name for a snail and refers to the way in which the stem climbs around trees. Cultivars of *H. helix* will tolerate very low temperatures but cannot take frost. During spring and summer they need a shady position; in winter they want as much light as possible. *Hedera helix* 'Pittsburgh', one of the first of the self-branching Ivies to be introduced, has small dark green leaves with lighter green veins. It is a vigorous grower. Like all ivies it can be propagated by cuttings in summer but takes a long time to root. *H. helix* 'Chicago' is similar to 'Pittsburgh', but has slightly larger leaves which are more cream than green.

H. helix sagittaefolia is another natural variety, which has leaves shaped like arrows. Although described as self-branching it does not produce sideshoots from every leaf joint and should be allowed to make quite a lot of growth before it is stopped, when about 4 inches should be removed. A variegated *H. h. sagittaefolia* which has strong markings and is quite a quick grower is also available. *H. helix* 'Little Diamond' is also variegated, with very small leaves that are practically without lobes and give the impression of being lance-shaped. They are dark grey-green with an ivory margin. The leaf is about 1 inch long and $\frac{1}{2}$ inch in width. This ivy is self-branching and a slow grower. *H. helix* 'Nielson' is not very different from 'Chicago', except that the leaves of the former grow closer together.

A plant which produces so many leaves that it never appears straggly is *H. helix* 'Golden Jubilee'. The leaves are small and yellow with a wide green margin. It is not self-branching so makes a thin plant and if two or three plants are put in a pot the effect will be more satisfactory. It is a very slow grower. Exposure to bright light encourages the leaves to show a more brilliant colour and to grow more vigorously. If the gold colour disappears it should be cut back to the first coloured leaf in spring. *H. helix* 'Glacier' is an unusual plant having greyish leaves with a cream margin, which becomes smaller as the leaves age. The general effect is silver grey. It is not self-branching but a rapid grower, producing a number of side shoots, and is very effective as a trailer. *H. helix* 'Green Ripple' is a self-branching plant, with remarkably pointed leaves resembling a vine leaf. The leaf has five lobes, about 2 inches long and $1\frac{1}{2}$ inches across. The two bottom lobes do not emerge until the leaf is well developed. The young leaves are bright green darkening with age.

The name *cristata* is given to a variety of *Hedera helix* because it means crested, and this *Hedera* has leaves which are fringed like those of parsley. They look nearly round but closer inspection shows they have seven lobes. Leaves are medium green when young becoming very dark with age. If it is allowed to reach a good size it will produce side-shoots. *H. helix marmorata* has leaves that are marbled with cream and green. It grows slowly, which is an advantage for a house plant, and is attractive. The leaf stalks are pink.

Hedera canariensis comes from the Canary Islands and, as might be expected, is not quite as hardy as the varieties of *H. helix*. They are still among the hardiest of house plants, however, and provided they are kept free from frost, will grow anywhere. They resent over-watering, particularly in winter, and it is better to wait until the leaves droop a little before watering. *H. canariensis foliis variegatis* can be translated as variegated Canary Island Ivy, and is a most delightful plant. The centre of the leaf is dark green and the edges are pale cream. No two leaves are identical. All these ivies are slow growers and it is best to put three rooted cuttings in each pot to make an effective plant. If over-watered, the leaves will turn yellow and fall off. An annual stopping seems to encourage more vigorous growth. *H. canariensis* 'Golden Leaf' is rather oddly named as the leaves are not golden, but bright green, with a lighter green patch in the centre, which in some lights can look yellowish. However, it is a most effective large house plant, especially at about 6 feet. The stem and leaf stalks are bright red. Feeding during the summer will improve growth of all varieties. Propagation is by cuttings that will root in soil or water.

Varieties of *Hedera helix: (from left to right)* 'Glacier', *cristata,* 'Golden Jubilee'

Pleione species are small with attractive flowers that grow well in a cold environment; a room with north-facing windows is ideal. This variety 'Indian Crocus' flowers in the spring.

Orchids

There are several reasons why orchids have not yet 'caught on' as house plants. They are a genus of great variety and, no doubt, will one day become extremely popular as indoor plants. Meanwhile many people are rather afraid of growing them, because they think that orchids need extremely high temperatures, are costly plants and are rather precious and delicate. In reality a great many orchids do not need higher temperatures than many other house plants. At temperatures above 4°C throughout the year, many of the cultivated orchids would grow easily out of doors. That they are relatively expensive is quite true, but orchids are not as expensive as they were formerly, and will no doubt get less expensive as culture increases.

Most orchids are epiphytes, dependent on organic matter washed down by rain from surrounding vegetation for nourishment. The plants attach themselves to trees by their roots, and most of them have a pseudo-bulb which stores water and nutriment during the dry season. This may be leafless or put forth several thick leathery, or light thin, leaves. From the base, or the axils of the leaves, the flowering stem grows out. After flowering the pseudo-bulb puts out shoots from its base which develop like itself, and in this way the plant multiplies. In some species flowering only takes place on a new bulb, and in others the older ones may bloom for several years. The epiphytes may be grown on a piece of bark, wood, or fibre, to which the plant is strapped or wired, with a pad of *Sphagnum* moss or *Osmunda* fibre to cover the roots. In due time the roots attach themselves and the binding can be removed. They should not be overwatered and the slabs can be hung by a hook in a sunny window, but not in direct sun.

Terrestrial orchids grow with roots in the ground like other plants and may, or may not, have a pseudo-bulb above ground level. The leaves are more attractive than those of the epiphytes and they are grown in pots in fibrous soils. The *Cypripedium* hybrid, 'Lady's Slipper', is an ideal terrestrial orchid for the amateur. It is getting cheaper and should soon be within the reach of all pockets. The waxy flower, in shades of brown, yellow, white and pale green, with a mass of

These orchids have sprays of flowers.
(Top) Odontoglossum and *Dendrobium*
(right); (left) Cymbidium

speckles, has a protruding lower slipper-petal which is highly polished. It flowers in winter and lasts, either on the plant or as a cut flower, for several weeks. It may need re-potting after flowering but, if the assistance of an orchid grower is available, his help should be sought as repotting orchids is a tricky business for a novice. If the plant is not cramped it can stay put for two to three years.

Baskets, preferably of teak, are good containers for these orchids and should be in partial shade; a pot can also be placed on a tray, or saucer, of moist pebbles and left in a north-west window. Cypripediums must be protected against hot sun, have fresh air in moderation, never be allowed in draughts and have a winter temperature of around 16° to 17°C. The plant can be watered lightly until it has settled down and, when growing freely, it can be sprayed and watered freely as it appreciates humidity. A uniform moisture should be kept throughout the pot, the soil being allowed to dry out between waterings. The foliage should be kept clean by sponging.

Cymbidium hybrids are also terrestrial orchids that do well in cool conditions and are not demanding over the matter of light. They produce their flowers on erect or branching spikes, which vary in height from 1 to 4 feet, according to species or hybrid. Some of the *Dendrobium* species can also be grown as house plants, although they need a little more heat than cymbidiums. *Dendrobium nobile* is a winter blooming orchid, which does not require a very high temperature and can do well in ordinary window light. Orchids are very economical to keep for they live on less than most plants and their rate of growth is very gradual. A high-nitrogen fertilizer should be used once a week, diluted to a quarter of the recommended strength, and every three months they should be watered for two weeks with an organic fertilizer. Most orchid pests can be killed by dipping the plant in mild malathion solutions.

The *Cypripedium* hybrid 'Lady's Slipper' bears single-stalked flowers

Pelargoniums

Flowers have their vogue. Pelargoniums were first taken up enthusiastically in Europe in the late eighteenth century and have never suffered a complete eclipse, although there have been times when the genus was out of favour. There is some confusion between the names 'pelargonium' and 'geranium'. The true *Geranium* is a cosmopolitan genus of which about eight species are native to South Africa, but are seldom cultivated as a garden plant. It is a member of the same family of the vegetable kingdom, named Geraniaceae, but the family was sub-divided for convenience of study by the French botanist L'Heritier who gave one of the sub-divisions the name *Pelargonium*. The earliest *Pelargonium* to be introduced to Europe was probably *P. zonale,* which was sent to Holland by a Dutch Governor of Cape Colony in 1609. Modern species have been classified into quite distinct types.

The Zonal pelargonium is one of the most popular cultivars (cultivated varieties) because it can usually be grown outside in summer. The colour range goes from white through pink, red, salmon, orange, magenta to picotee and fancy, while the

Zonal pelargonium 'Carnival' *(below)* and 'Lady of Spain' *(right)*

Unique hybrid 'Scarlet Pet' *(above)* and Zonal pelargonium 'Mrs Ward' *(left)*

ivy-leaved flowers continue the colour range to purple. Many scents and essences are distilled from the plants and the leaves of many are esculent and are used for culinary purposes and for garnishing. Zonal pelargoniums, known so often simply as 'geraniums' derive principally from that sub-genus *Ciconium*. They are partly shrubby and partly succulent; the wild forms straggle somewhat, as many of their cultivated descendants will do if not discouraged. The root system is fibrous. The leaves are large, 3 to 4 inches in diameter and roughly circular, except where they are attached to the stem, where they are cordate. In its single state the Zonal pelargonium has five petals, of which the upper two are generally smaller than the lower three. A curious furling of the petals, so that they have a quill-like appearance, gives a 'cactus flowered' sub-group. In size, blooms vary from nearly 3 inches to less than $\frac{1}{4}$ inch. The flowers are borne in umbels, the number of florets in a truss may be four or a hundred. Habit is sometimes erect, sometimes almost prostrate, sometimes very large, reaching a height of 6 to 7 feet, sometimes miniature, not exceeding a few inches.

The Regal pelargoniums are mostly grown in greenhouses and plant rooms. Their popularity has been of longer standing than the Zonal pelargoniums but because they are less successful as garden plants they are not so extensively grown. They are more shrubby and their leaves are unzoned, generally a darker green, much less fleshy and usually toothed. Instead of being held more or less flat as is the Zonal, the leaf of the Regal is often cupped. The basic colour of the Regal pelargonium is mauve and a further distinction is the marking of the petals, which are blotched, streaked and striped. They do not normally bloom for so long a period. There are very large growing kinds such as 'Corisbrooke', which has fringed, pinky-mauve flowers and dwarf, bushy types such as 'Sancho Panza'. Quite large plants may be grown to cover walls on verandahs and plant rooms. During the winter they require a temperature of 7° to 10°C and should be watered very sparingly.

Ivy-leaved pelargoniums stem from the species *P. peltatum,* a native of South Africa. They are of shrubby character, with weak straggly

Leaves of variegated types of *Pelargonium*

'Mrs Henry Cox'

'The Boar'

'Distinction'

Double-flowered Zonal
pelargoniums

'La France'

'Royal Purple'

'Love'

branches and shoots up to 3 feet long, carrying ivy-shaped, rather fleshy green leaves, 2 to 3 inches across. The heads of flowers are on 3 to 4 inch stalks from the leaf axil in summer. There are several selected forms such as 'Mme Crousse' which has pale pink, double flowers, 'L'Elegante' which has single, white, purple-feathered flowers and 'Abel Carriers' with double, tyrian-purple flowers. They are good plants for pedestals, hanging baskets, or as climbers. Cultural needs are similar to those of Zonal pelargoniums, and they also flower in summer.

Scented-leaved pelargoniums make delightful pot plants that can be grown indoors all the year. The flowers are hardly spectacular, but the leaves have a diversity of shape and perfume which is extremely appealing. *P. crispum lactifolia* has a fruity, orange scent and medium-sized leaves. *P. mellisimum* has tri-lobed, lemon-scented leaves and *P. nervosum* deep green, lime-scented leaves with trailing branches. A strong rose scent is provided by *P. graveolens* 'Lady Plymouth' and an apricot scent by *P. scabrum*. The dark glossy,

'Cladius' a miniature
black-leaved pelargonium

pointed leaves are deeply toothed, and the large flowers are rose-coloured. *P. tomentosum* has large hairy, heart-shaped leaves, redolent of peppermint. They require similar treatment to Zonal pelargoniums and propagating by cutting is easy, especially in spring and summer.

Coloured leaves have been bred from Zonal pelargoniums and in these forms, too, the flowers are less conspicuous and more sparingly produced. There are golden leaves which explain themselves and are provided by 'Robert Fish', which has pale yellow leaves and orange-scarlet flowers, and 'Beth Watts' with pale golden leaves, pale pink flowers. Butterfly leaves have an irregular wing shape in the middle of the leaf. The 'butterfly' is usually a lighter colour than the body of the leaf; less common is the reverse arrangement. 'Happy Thought' has green leaves, white or cream butterfly and crimson flowers. 'Crystal Palace Gem' has yellow-green leaves, green butterfly and small rose-pink flowers. Bi-colour leaves can be seen on 'Black Cox' which has dark green leaves, zoned in black and rose flowers. 'Bronze Corrine' has a chestnut zone on golden ground and bright scarlet flowers. 'Crampel Master' has three-colour leaves of olive-green with a white centre streaked with gold. It has a pale green stem, streaked dark green, and vermilion flowers. So far this is the only three-colour variation on the market. 'Mrs. Henry Cox' has four-colour leaves of pale gold, marked erratically with purple, red, cream and green. The flowers are rose-coloured. 'Sophie Dumaresque' has a broad zone suffused with bronze and crimson and bordered with a flame colour. It has red flowers.

The group called Uniques are most nearly related to the Regals. Their growth is shrubby and somewhat straggly, woody rather than succulent, their leaves are irregularly and deeply cut, and usually of a deeper green. The colour range at present contains few varieties; white, pink, scarlet, crimson and deep purple-mauve. They are not really showy enough for garden work and it is as plants for the windowsill or plant room that they are at their best.

Angel pelargoniums seldom exceed 10 inches and their flowers are large in relation to the size of the plant, the petals broadly obovate which gives the flower a round, full face of overlapping petals. They make thick little bushes of slender herbaceous branches, well covered with small leaves and are excellent wherever there is sufficient light.

Single-flowered pelargoniums: *(left)* Regal pelargonium 'Grand Slam' *(right)* Zonal pelargonium 'Millfield Rival' *(bottom)* Regal pelargonium 'Comptesse de Choiseul'

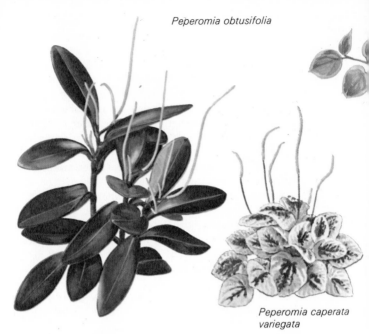

Peperomia obtusifolia

Peperomia caperata variegata

Pepper and arrowroot families

The pepper family is not a large one, and only two of the genera are in general cultivation, one of these is the genus *Piper* and the other is the genus *Peperomia;* most of the species are found in central and tropical South America. All the house plant peperomias are American in origin. In a wild state they are found growing in very shallow soil or more frequently in the moss at the base of a tree or in the hollows between branches. They are not epiphytic but they give an appearance of being so, and cannot absorb much nourishment. However, plants will tolerate conditions in the wild that they cannot do in the artificial state of cultivation. The root system of peperomias is never very extensive. They are placed in small pots and not potted-on until absolutely necessary. There is no need to worry about the plants becoming pot-bound. The one constant feature of the peperomias, although they vary in habit and leaf-shape, is the inflorescence. This is a thin spike resembling the spadix of a small arum. It is generally white or

Peperomia argyreia

cream in colour, not particularly striking, but contrasts well
with the curved leaves that most peperomias possess. They
require very infrequent watering, with tepid water and
occasional spraying will lessen the risk of Red Spider. Temperatures should not fall below 10°C.

Peperomia caperata variegata is distinguished by the heart-
shaped leaves of cream and green and the cream flower spikes.
The plant never grows very large. *Peperomia magnoliaefolia* is
a sturdy shrubby little plant with compact growth and
frequent side shoots. The leaves are about 2 inches long and
$1\frac{3}{4}$ inches across. New leaves have a thin grey-green streak in
the centre and wide cream edges, which fade to pale green as
the leaf ages. Propagation is by leaf cuttings. *P. obtusifolia* is a
handsome plant that will eventually reach a foot in height.
The leaves are over 4 inches long and 2 inches wide, and are
dark green with a purple edge. They are thick and fleshy and
the plant tolerates dry conditions for a long time. Propagation
is by stem cuttings. *P. argyreia,* the silver Peperomia, has thick

Leaf of *Calathea ornata (left)* and *Maranta leuconeura massangeana*

smooth leaves, nearly round, marked in alternate bands of silver and dark green. A mature leaf is 4 inches long and 3 inches across. It dislikes draughts, and will rot if over watered. *P. scandens* is a most effective trailer and will extend 4 to 5 feet if allowed. The variegated variety is the one that is obtainable commercially. The leaves are small, about 2 inches in length and $1\frac{3}{4}$ inches across. Young leaves are pale green with a cream border, but as they mature the green spreads and the amount of cream is diminished. The main stem is green, the petioles flushed with pink. It is difficult to grow in its early stages, it is much easier when fairly sizeable.

The arrowroot plants belong to the family Marantaceae. The majority of them come from South America, particularly Brazil. They need a warm, moist atmosphere and in summer it is best to keep them in a double pot, with absorbent material packed between the inner and outer pots, which can be moistened with warm water. The temperature should not be allowed to drop below 10°C, preferably 15°C. All Marantaceae

Calathea zebrina

Maranta leuconeura kerchoveana

are shade lovers, and should be kept on the damp side. Propagation is by division when repotting.

Calathea mackoyana, also known as *Maranta mackoyana*, is known in the United States as the 'Peacock Plant' and has quite large oblong-oval leaves. These are silver-green, with markings of dark green along the principal veins; on the underside the markings are reddish purple. It will eventually grow to a height of 3 feet. *Calathea zebrina*, or 'Zebra Plant', is another striking *Calathea* with long, lance-shaped leaves of deep emerald green, striped with even darker green on the surface, and purple beneath. In *C. ornata* the leaves are broadly ovate, almost purple-green in colour, etched with fine, pale pink lines between the lateral veins and deep purple beneath. As a house plant it grows up to 2 feet. All the calatheas like a humid, warm, well-lit position that is out of direct sunlight. Watering should be done freely in summer and the leaves washed regularly. In winter soil should be just moist. Propagation is by division when repotting.

Calathea makoyana

Saintpaulias (African violets)

The modern history of the saintpaulia began with its discovery towards the end of the last century by the District Governor of Usambara in East Africa. He sent seeds to his father, who in his turn brought them to the notice of the Director of the Royal Botanic Gardens at Herrenhausen, who issued the description of the species and named it *Saintpaulia ionantha*.

In the natural state, these plants root in the rock crevices where humus has gathered. A certain amount of shade is present in these places, which gives an idea of the conditions the plants like; which is plenty of light, but not direct sunshine, with humidity and warmth. They are becoming more popular with the advent of better home heating, although they have been of interest to commercial growers in the United States for nearly forty years.

Saintpaulias have a reputation for being difficult plants to grow. In actual fact, the saintpaulia is no more difficult than many other house plants and it is an interesting plant to grow, easy to propagate and the flowers and leaves are both attractive. The leaves are broadly oval, darkish green and somewhat

Varieties of *Saintpaulia*

'San Mateo'

'Peak of Pink'

'White Rhapsody'

African violets are very
popular for use in plant
groups; combined here
with *Chlorophytum* and a
variegated ivy

hairy. They are produced on short stout stalks from the base
that spread flatly to form a background for the violet-blue,
two-lipped flowers. The upper lip is broken into two lobes
that are much smaller than the lower, which has three lobes,
and there is a centre of orange-yellow stamens. The flowers are
borne in loose cymes on stalks 3 to 4 inches long. There are now
many varieties in shades of blue, purple, pink, white and
almost red, and there are double-flowering forms of even
greater beauty.

It is a good plan to purchase a first stock of plants in the
early summer when house conditions are most likely to be
favourable. Sunlight in the early morning or evening will do
them no harm and, in summer, fine mesh net curtains will
probably provide sufficient shade. In winter house plants
should never be left between drawn curtains and the window
pane, for that is the coldest part of the room. Room temperature

should be a minimum of 10°C and it is preferable to water at a regular temperature of around 12°C to 15°C. It is fluctuation in temperature that does the harm.

Another cause of damage is the combination of high temperature and a dry atmosphere. African violets do not mind dryness around the roots, providing they are in a humid atmosphere, but keeping the soil moist is not sufficient to provide humidity around the plant. It is far better to keep the roots of the plant on the dry side as overwatering will only cause them to rot. Steps must, therefore, be taken to provide

this humid atmosphere, while at the same time keeping the plant soil only slightly moist.

Inside the house humidity can be provided by placing the pots of saintpaulias on a bed of constantly moist pebbles and gravel in a waterproof tray. Individual pots can be stood on damp pebbles in a saucer. A pot of saintpaulias may be put into a larger container and the space between the two packed with peat or *Sphagnum* moss, which has already been well soaked, and is afterwards kept moist. These plants also revel in steam and are good plants for a warm bathroom. Pots must never be allowed to stand in water for the roots will certainly start to rot. As a general rule you will find that no feeding is required for African violets for at least a year after buying them. If they are not repotted in the second year, an occasional dose of liquid feed during the summer months may be given, but this should only be in small quantities at rather long intervals, say every three to four weeks. Propagation is quite easily carried out, either by seed or by leaf cuttings.

Leaf cuttings are the easiest method and ensures that the resultant plants are the same as the plant that supplied the cuttings. A leaf from the plant you wish to propagate, together

Humidity provided for African violets by a goldfish bowl *(left)* that can be closed with glass or plastic. *Sphagnum* moss conceals the flowerpot *(Right and below)* method of providing humidity by filling space between pots with moist peat or moss

with its stem, should be removed and inserted shallowly into some propagating medium. Equal quantities of peat and sharp sand make a satisfactory mixture; or vermiculite, or pure sharp sand can be used. Leaves from the middle tier of leaves are usually suitable. They should be removed carefully with a sharp knife and trimmed square across the end of the stalk so that there is about 1 inch of stalk left. The trimmed cutting should be dried off for about an hour before insertion into the rooting medium, then buried about $\frac{1}{4}$ inch deep. An upturned jam jar over each pot conserves moisture and prevents the compost drying out. Late spring and early summer are the best time to propagate by leaf cuttings, during colder weather a propagating case, with bottom heat, would be necessary.

A simple method of increasing stock, where no special facilities are available for propagation, is by filling a large jam jar to the brim with rain water, tying paper over the top and making three or four holes in the paper. A good selected leaf should be inserted into each hole, poking the stems down well so that the leaf blade is only just clear of the paper. It can be topped up with rain water if necessary, making sure the water used is the same temperature as that already in the jar. The jar must be stood in a window where there is plenty of light but no direct sun and within about six weeks white roots will be noticed coming out from the bottom of the stem. A little later very small leaves will be seen at the base of the leaf blade. As soon as the largest of these new leaves is about $\frac{1}{2}$ inch high the leaf cuttings should be potted up separately, using a fairly rich compost, into 2 inch pots, very well crocked.

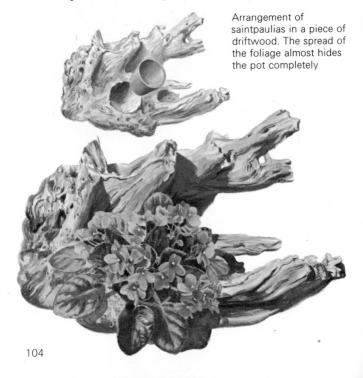

Arrangement of saintpaulias in a piece of driftwood. The spread of the foliage almost hides the pot completely

Popular varieties of saint-paulias are: 'Blue Boy', which has large single violet flowers; 'Blue Girl' distinguished by the scalloped edges of its leaves and which also has single, violet flowers; 'Pink Beauty' with single pink flowers; 'White Lady' with single flowers that are white as the name implies. Although the single saintpaulias are more attractive to many people, they tend to drop their flowers more quickly whereas the double hold their flowers until they fade. When over, the double flowers can be removed with a pair of scissors otherwise they may rot and the rot spread down the flower stems to the leaves and body of the plant. Double varieties recommended are blue 'Double Delight', pink 'Rococo', mauve-violet 'Red Comet', white 'White Pride' and pale mauve 'Lacy Lavender'. They are seldom sold by name, however, except by the specialist nurseries, so the best points to look for when selecting plants are good dark foliage and thick flower stems.

Two of the many varieties of the *Saintpaulia* that can be found on sale. Plants are rarely sold by name and the best points to look for when selecting them are dark foliage and thick flower stems.

Tradescantias

These are very easily grown plants and will only get into a poor condition if they are given no attention at all. Some species are quite hardy and can be grown outside, but the most popular plants are for indoor growth. *Tradescantia fluminensis*, commonly known as the 'Wandering Jew' or 'Wandering Sailor', is the one most usually seen. *Tradescantia fluminensis tricolor* is a popular variety, as is *Tradescantia fluminensis* 'New Silver'. If these plants are given a lot of light then some pink or mauve can often be seen in the foliage. They grow quickly and will produce long trailing stems that should be cut back drastically to induce bushiness. *Tradescantia albiflora* is an extremely similar, although slightly smaller, plant to *Tradescantia fluminensis*.

Tradescantia blossfeldiana grows upright on a stiffer stem. Thicker stems are hairy and the leaves have a similar hairy covering in some of the varieties. The undersides of

(From top to bottom)
Tradescantia fluminensis tricolor,
Setcreasea purpurea,
Tradescantia blossfeldiana,
Tradescantia blossfeldiana
tricolor

older leaves of this species are purple but there are many varieties, some of which present an almost complete purple appearance *T. blossfeldiana tricolor* is one of the more popular varieties. *Tradescantia reginae* also grows erect, with leaves that are about 6 inches in length. These are light green in colour with dark green bands and purple on the underside.

All *Tradescantia* shoots can be used as cuttings and rooted in a sandy soil during the summer months. They should be given plenty of water in summer, less in winter and should always be stood in a good light to preserve the variegated appearance. Sometimes rapid growth results in plain green shoots, which should be cut out whenever they appear. Plants can generally withstand some draughts although, preferably, they should always be kept warm. They can be grown in houses with gas central heating and growth improves with feeding during the summer months. If the air is too dry, it may cause lower leaves to shrivel and a light spraying with water at room temperature is beneficial.

Tradescantias are sometimes confused with species of *Zebrina* and *Setcreasea*. *Zebrina pendula* is very similar to *Tradescantia fluminensis,* but the leaves are slightly larger, thicker and coloured more vividly. It grows more slowly than tradescantias and dislikes direct heat. *Setcreasea* are similar in shape to *Zebrina* and *S. purpurea* or 'Purple Heart', has elongated leaves of a purple-red. They will not grow with so little attention, needing more warmth and good light. Both of these genera will propagate easily from cuttings.

Tradescantia 'New Silver'

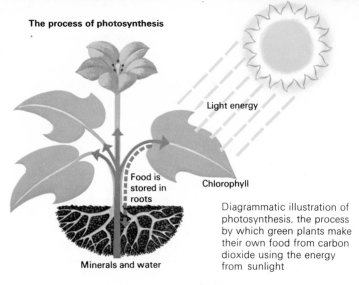

The process of photosynthesis

Light energy

Food is stored in roots

Chlorophyll

Minerals and water

Diagrammatic illustration of photosynthesis, the process by which green plants make their own food from carbon dioxide using the energy from sunlight

GENERAL CARE OF HOUSE PLANTS

The general care of house plants is largely a matter of common sense and cleanliness is essential. The air is full of grime and dust, even in the country, and in built-up areas it is even more important to give plants a regular clean, otherwise, if these deposits accumulate, their breathing will become clogged and this can prove fatal. A healthy plant bought from a reliable nursery should be self-supporting and not pot-bound, so it will not need supplementary feeding for two to three months.

The sudden transition from a humid greenhouse to the aridity of a heated living-room is a major change in growing conditions. To help overcome this, plants should be purchased, if possible, during the spring and summer months. This will give plants a chance to adapt themselves to their new environment without the added discomfort of the dry air which usually accompanies artificial heat. Leaves may start to turn yellow and fall off a few days after plants are received but this is usually only a passing phase that will be soon overcome providing the plants are not over watered, are given plenty of fresh air but *not* draughts, and good light but *not* direct sunlight. Due attention must also be given to pest fighting, pruning and training.

Plants which require full light

Most 'florist's' plants such as *Azalea*, chrysanthemums, cinerarias, *Fuchsia*, hyacinths, lilies, primulas, tulips and all variegated plants. Begonias, *Coleus*, *Codiaeum*, and poinsettias should be shaded from direct sunlight, while *Impatiens* and pelargoniums should be stood in full sun

Plants which need moderately good light

Aechmea, most bromeliads, calatheas, the draceanas, Maidenhair Fern, marantas, palms and *Peperomia*

(Above) Primula sinensis, the Chinese Primula, *(left) Draceana sandersi*, and *(below) Araucaria excelsa*, the Norfolk Island Pine a tough house plant that grows quickly

Plants that will tolerate low light

Generally plants that are a deep dark green in colour and all dark green ferns. Also *Aspidistra*, *Araucaria*, *Cissus*, *Cryptanthus*, diffenbachias, *Ficus elastica*, and sansevierias.

Dwarf poinsettias placed under a lamp to give them sufficient light. Humidity is provided by standing the plants on a metal tray of gravel, kept permanently moist

Light requirements

All green plants respond to light since it regulates their growth. Up to a certain point, the more light a plant receives in intensity and duration, the greater the need for water, warmth and nutrients. Too much, especially direct sunlight, overtaxes the plant and is apt to lead to wilting and scorching, too little forces weak pallid growth, encouraging vegetative growth at the expense of flowers. All green plants grown indoors turn their leaves to the source of light, to present the maximum surface area to the light rays. The richer and deeper the green, the more able is the plant to absorb light and the more adaptable it is to shade. The tendency of plants to grow one-sidedly towards the light can be corrected by turning the plant around, not abruptly, but regularly and gradually. The higher the temperature, within reason, the more light a plant will need and it is the low light intensity of winter, rather than the low temperature, that limits the growth of plants during the winter months. Under central heating conditions the tendency is to maintain temperatures above the ideal for plants in the winter light available.

Much experimenting has been taking place for many years with the use of artificial light to supplement natural light for plant culture, and nowadays the use of high pressure mercury vapour lamps for growing plants is quite widespread commercially, although unsuitable for homes. The best lamp for this purpose is a fluorescent tube and reflector, which arranged suitably, produces a good effect while improving the quality and vigour of the plants. These lamps should be installed by an electrician, and all metal parts efficiently earthed. The ordinary 4 feet by 40 watt, warm white or daylight tubes are most suitable. The tube must be only 10 to 12 inches above the foliage and although they do not appear to dissipate much heat, the loss of humidity from the plants beneath must be replaced. There are a number of manufactured cabinets that will hold plants but existing troughs can be adapted.

A plant display case, or propagating case in some instances, fitted with artificial light. A similar case could easily be made from wood. A standard-sized reflector fluorescent light fitting is mounted at the apex, the glass front is removable and there is a panel cut in the base to enable insertion of a low-powered heater if so desired.

Supports for climbing plants

The type of support used for climbing plants grown in the house is extremely important. It should be well chosen, because much depends on it. It can give a suitable natural support that will make a climber look attractive or it can appear incongruous and awkward.

Moss sticks are simple to make using either $2\frac{1}{2}$ or 3 feet wide, $\frac{1}{4}$ inch square plastic mesh, of which a 10 inch wide strip will be needed. This should be rolled into a cylinder, overlapping the edges about $\frac{3}{4}$ inch and fastening it with strands of wire at about 4 inch intervals. About 2 inches of gravel should be put into a tub, or large pot, for drainage and two small flat sticks pushed through the bottom of the cylinder, at

Philodendron scandens, the easily grown climber, growing around a moss stick *(left)*. *(Opposite)* the method of making a moss stick: suitable wire is bent round to form a cylinder and fastened securely; sticks pushed through the base will keep the stick firm in a pot or tub; the stick is most easily filled with the aid of a paper funnel; plants are placed at appropriate intervals around the base and pinned to the stick as desired.

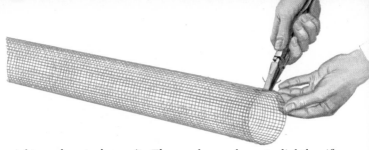

right angles, to brace it. The mesh can be cut slightly, if necessary, to enable the sticks to be slipped in, and standard potting mixtures used to fill the tub. The cylinder can be filled with a mixture of half peat or shredded moss and half vermiculite or perlite. If peat or moss is used it should be soaked overnight to dampen it properly. The cylinder is most easily filled with the aid of a paper funnel, stopping at intervals during filling to press the mixture down firmly with the aid of a short broom handle, until the cylinder is full.

The plants chosen to grow against the moss stick could be *Philodendron, Hedera canariensis, Scindapsus,* or any other attractive climber, and should be firmly placed in the tub, using three to five plants for an arrangement of this size. Only one or two plants should be used for a smaller stick in a smaller pot. The roots must be covered to within an inch of the rim to allow for watering. The climbers can be trained to grow in a spiral around the moss stick by pinning their branches to the stick with hairpins inserted at a sharp angle. The stick should be watered daily to keep it damp, and when the tub is watered it can be filled to the brim and allowed to settle. This

should be continued until it drains out at the bottom, but the surface must have dried out before it is re-watered.

Morning Glories and other similar plants that climb by twining, can be given three light pieces of bamboo to twine around. These can be put in the pot itself at regular intervals round the edge. About half-way up the length of the stakes a hoop can be installed. An embroidery hoop of sufficient size will do and it should be fastened to each stake. The tops of the stakes should then be brought together and tied firmly.

There are many variations of this theme of support. Pliable canes can be bent over a pot to give one or more looped supports, or tied to give a trellis or ladder effect. This latter form of support is commonly seen in arrangements of members of the ivy family but is suitable for all climbers. In many places, ready made plastic supports can be bought from gardening centres. Plastic-covered wire can also often be used and is

(Top) canes and wire form a support for *Ipomea. (Right)* some of the many types of cane and wire support that can be made for house plants

frequently bent into many attractive shapes. Care should be taken to see that ordinary wire, if used, does not rust.

Sometimes a simple wood trellis is used, together with climbers, as a room divider. They are usually constructed with a wooden base of about 1¼ inch thick material of whatever length is required. The trellis is attached to this by means of wooden uprights reinforced by angle irons.

On these bases, troughs or pots containing the climbers can be stood. The plants can be unobtrusively attached with fine string to the trellis background here and there and then left to find their own way with a minimum of attention. In Denmark much use is made of string and drawing pins which are fixed directly to the walls, but this is really not to be recommended. The plants are apt to get out of control and much of their distinction is lost in a tangle of jungle.

Climbing plants on a trellis that could be used as a room divider. The trellis can be easily constructed to the desired size by an amateur. The two plants are *Fatshedera lizei*, which is a cross between a *Fatsia* and an ivy and will tolerate most household conditions, and *Rhoicissus rhomboidea (right)*

Containers for house plants

The battle between clay and glazed pots has raged for many years and will probably continue to do so. Clay pots have an unbeatable porous quality and a reasonable price, the glazed pots retain moisture better and can be had in all shapes, colours, and sizes. Sometimes the colour and designs compete with the plant for attention, which is unfortunate.

Providing the pot has a drainage hole the choice is a personal matter. There are pot holders in great variety into which a clay pot can be slipped and, if so wished, clay pots can be painted with flat oil, or emulsion paint in white, pale green, grey or any other colour to tone with the surroundings. It must be remembered, however, that pots treated in this way become less porous and plants will require more attention from the watering can.

Soup tureens and copper or brass troughs make excellent outer containers for pots of house plants that like extra humidity. They can be packed around with damp peat or moss and stood on saucers of wet pebbles, although the bottom of the pot should not be allowed to touch the water. Table trolleys on wheels are useful too. They can be moved away from the window on a cold night, or out of range of the midday summer sun. Jardinieres, especially the white-painted, curly Victorian ones are always attractive, especially for pelargoniums. Four, five or six tier saucepan stands, suitably painted, make good holders for a small number of pots. Drip catchers must always be considered and, for these, painted tins of a suitable size with low sides, or the odd saucer are always useful.

Pedestals, wooden or wrought iron, are useful for mixtures of plants, including some of the trailing ones. There are many osier and cane shapes available and small pieces of furniture such as log boxes, wine coolers, tea pots or tantalus cases can be used, but careful selection of plants will have to be made before they are filled. In some cases the house plants will need lifting within the container, probably by nothing more complicated than an upturned flower pot.

Various containers for house plants. *(Opposite)* the box and the urn are made from glass-fibre and have been finished to resemble the historic lead originals of which they are copies; the attractive conical container is in simulated stone. *(Below)* household articles that would readily adapt as plant containers

Although many household items can be converted into suitable containers for house plants and there are also many articles on the market that can be used, some people prefer to make their own containers. Cane baskets of any required size can be made to suit any particular situation. Wooden bases and various thicknesses of cane can be bought from a handicraft store. The container can then be made into a variety of shapes, to stand or hang. Troughs, or other wooden containers, can be made to fit alcoves, shelves, or window-sills.

When house plants are stood in wooden or metal containers without a drip tray or saucer beneath them, care should be taken when watering. The plant should be removed and only returned after it has been given a thorough watering and the pot base is dry. Otherwise wood will rot and metal will rust. When climb-

(Top) the display of *Sansevieria, Chlorophytum,* and a *Philodendron* is produced by concealing the individual plant pots' in a chip basket. Other types of wooden fruit baskets can also be used. *(Left)* other types of plant pot disguisers

ing plants are grown in basketwork it is impossible to remove them once they have established themselves and some form of protective drip tray should be incorporated if watering is to be carried out satisfactorily.

It is always helpful to put plant pots inside another container, often decorative, because this will cut down evaporation from the pot surface. If the space between the two can be filled with some water-absorbing material, the roots will be able to obtain much of the moisture they need through the porous sides or the base hole.

There is much room for thought as to the means of displaying plants and a constant search for unusual containers will often yield some very attractive results. If plants are kept in their pots inside their containers, it will be possible to give them individual attention and watering. Group effects can easily be camouflaged with moss.

These two plant holders are made of cane and are often made at home to suit specific requirements. Because the plants usually trail or climb around their containers it is impossible to remove them for watering and a drip tray should be incorporated

Tools

The house plant gardener does not require a tool shed. The few implements that are necessary are largely a matter of personal choice and can often be adapted from ordinary household items.

A fork of some kind is essential. The old two-prong kitchen variety is quite suitable but the prongs should be slightly blunted. It is used to keep the top soil open, preventing the soil packing down with watering and permitting the passage of air to the roots. A small trowel is necessary for filling troughs and other containers and a potting stick or dibble is used to make the appropriate size holes when planting all but the largest plants. These items can be bought at any gardening shop and some places sell special miniature sets of tools especially for the house plant gardener.

The selection of tools should also include a sharp knife, perhaps the old gardener's penknife variety or a modern pruning knife, as well as some small sharp secateurs that can be used for pruning and cutting. A finely nozzled syringe for spraying is also quite an important item and, if plants are

long-spouted watering can

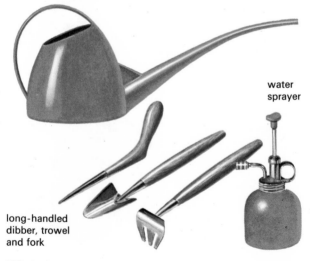

water sprayer

long-handled
dibber, trowel
and fork

given a regular spray, cleaning will be less difficult. When cleaning is necessary, a large, soft paintbrush is suitable for brushing most types of leaf. Sprays can also be used for insecticides and foliar foodstuffs but should be labeled carefully and their use never confused.

A polythene watering can with a long narrow spout is the best watering utensil because the flow can be directed beneath the foliage and away from the vulnerable crown of the plant. Rainwater at room temperature is the best medium and the correct temperature is most easily obtained by keeping a full can in the room. Many other articles can be added as they are found desirable and could include a sieve for sifting soil for small pots, plant labels, twine, canes and stakes and gardening gloves or lined rubber gloves.

If a suitable basket can be obtained to hold all these items it will make for tidiness and save time. There is nothing more infuriating than having to search for a tool that is required for a certain trivial job at a certain moment. A cloth for mopping up the overflow resulting from over-zealous watering will probably also find its way into the tool basket.

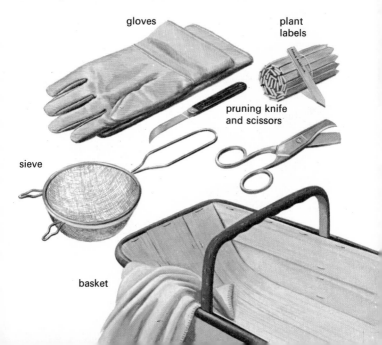

gloves

plant labels

pruning knife and scissors

sieve

basket

Pruning and training

House plants often need pruning in the interest of shapeliness, and for curbing untidy and weak growth. This should only be carried out when the plants have become well-rooted and are making active growth.

When it is necessary to remove weak shoot growth or to cut back a plant the best time of year to do it is the latter half of spring. Unwanted growth should be cut out right at its base, or at the junction with an older stem from which new growth is desired. Many plants such as pileas and aphelandras lose most of their leaves in winter. If this does happen they should be cut back to about 2 inches above the soil level. New growths should then begin from this base.

In the case of climbing plants, bushy growth can be encouraged by the simple process of 'stopping' or 'pinching out' the growing tips of shoots just above a leaf. Ivies and climbing philodendrons are treated in this

Should a *Ficus* become inconveniently tall, it can be shortened to a more suitable height by trimming off the central stem just above a leaf junction.

way. If climbers are being trained in any particular direction, then unwanted shoots can also be cut back.

Some house plants are really trees and may need curtailment in time. This is frequently the case with such plants as *Ficus elastica* and *Grevillea robusta*. These can be induced to branch by shortening them in spring. Flowering plants, which form their buds on new growth each year, can be pruned quite hard in the spring but those that form their buds on older growth need very little pruning beyond the cutting back of occasional shoots to keep a shapely appearance. Some of the more decorative foliage plants, such as *Coleus*, produce insignificant flowers which should be pinched out to prevent leaf loss after flowering.

Climbing plants such as *Cissus*, and trailing plants such as *Tradescantia*, can be kept neat by having their growing points stopped from time to time, when necessary, during the growing season. Some plants may tend to bleed after being cut and should be dressed with a proprietary antiseptic.

Some variegated plants, like the *Tradescantia (below)* grow all-green shoots occasionally. These should be pinched out when they occur. Some plants like the *Coleus* should have their insignificant flowers pinched out to preserve the foliage.

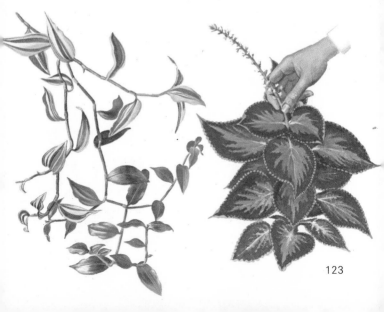

Feeding

A healthy plant bought from a shop or nursery should be self-sufficient for at least three months. The basic mixture in which it is planted should contain the right mineral salts and the plant should not be pot-bound. If this is the case, the soil will require a minimum of care for some time.

It must be remembered that supplementary feeding can be dangerous. Sick or water-logged plants, if fed, will merely have their troubles accentuated but a pot-bound plant, or a rapid grower, probably needs a pick-me-up. The soil should be moist before feeding and should be watered after feeding to avoid any risk of burning the sensitive rootlets with the stimulant that has been decided upon.

Weak manure is, of course, an excellent fertilizer. One cupfull of dried cow manure put into a bag and suspended in a gallon of water for about four weeks is a very suitable liquid food, but even if it is obtainable, which is doubt-

(From top to bottom) the three methods of feeding plants: by pills or tablets; by powder; by liquid fertilizer

A newly purchased plant will not require any fertilizer for the first few months after it is bought. It should just be given the correct amount of light and water. The plant is *Pilea cadieri*.

ful for occupants of a flat, it does have a scent which is certainly not the favourite of most people. There are, fortunately, a number of useful, handy, stimulants – fertilizers in granular or powder form – such as bone meal or plant tablets, although it is doubtful whether any of these can give such an even performance as a liquid feed. There are many suitable proprietary brands on the market today.

A complete fertilizer suits most plants and will contain nitrogen, phosphorus and potash. Nitrogen promotes foliage growth and a good green colouring. Phosphates are helpful in assisting in the formation of flowers, fruits, seeds and roots. Potash helps plants to resist disease, while at the same time strengthening growth. On no account should a sick plant or a new arrival be fed; nor a newly potted plant. A plant that is resting should not be fed and most plants rest during the winter season. Feeding should begin when the plant starts into

Overfeeding and overwatering can cause the leaves to turn yellow *(left)*. *(Below)* diagram of a self-watering bowl and wick

growth and should go on during the spring and summer. Plants should not be over-fed and the instructions on the packet should be followed very carefully. A little less fertilizer should be given rather than a little more and *all* fresh manure must be avoided. Manure must have been well decayed for a long time, otherwise it will burn plant roots.

The composts that are used for growing house plants have been greatly simplified during recent years. There used to be a special mixture for practically every different pot plant but now, thanks to the John Innes Horticultural Institute, standard mixtures have been evolved. These can be used to serve a

Various potting mediums

wide range of plants and, unless house plants are grown on a fairly large scale, it is much easier to buy compost ready mixed from a reliable supplier.

Some house plants such as dieffenbachias, philodendrons and monsteras, do require special composts. These plants have soft fleshy roots and need a porous open growing medium that is a mixture of two parts fibrous loam, two parts peat and one part sharp sand. Most of the bromeliads that are grown as house plants are epiphytes and in their natural surroundings grow on the branches of trees. These require a compost that is almost entirely organic matter since they are watered through the cup-like 'vase' in the centre of the plant, not at the roots. A good mixture is made of equal parts fibrous loam, flaky leaf mould, rough peat, and silver sand. It is also possible to grow house plants in vermiculite which has a perfect texture for house plant roots but contains no nutrients, so the plants have to be fed fairly often.

It is impossible to give any hard and fast rules for watering but, basically, soil should be allowed to become almost dry before more water is given, although the soil should never be allowed to dry out entirely. The surface of the soil often is

Bromeliads and philodendrons
(right) are two of the many
plants requiring special composts

misleadingly dry and it should be scraped about $\frac{1}{2}$ inch down to see the true nature of the soil.

Overwatering is far more dangerous than too little watering, although good drainage will reduce this danger. Most plants need watering about two to three times a week in summer, only once a week in winter. A plant that must be left for a few weeks can be thoroughly soaked and put in a polythene bag, tying the bag at soil level around the plant. A thin wick of tape leading to the pots from another vessel is a good self-watering method that can also be adopted.

The plant is held and compost poured around the roots

It should be pressed firm with the fingers

Watering in — not to be done again until the plant dries out

Potting a new plant, a process known as potting up

Propagation

The living functions of perennial plants never cease entirely but there is a time when they are at their lowest ebb and the plants enjoy a rest period. The rest period is one when a plant slowly girds itself by maturing changes for a renewal of active growth. As the plants begin to awaken from their rest period, during which time they need very little or no water and lower temperatures than when in full growth, it is a good time to repot old-established plants.

Repotting operations are the same for young or older plants. The plant itself should be in soil on the dry side so that it can be easily dislodged from its present pot. A clean pot is essential. Pots greened from previous use should be soaked in a bucket of potassium permanganate ($\frac{1}{4}$ ounce per gallon of water) overnight, then scrubbed. If new clay or absorbent pots are used, they should be soaked for twenty-four hours beforehand. There is nothing to be gained by giving a plant a pot larger than it needs, for this leads to water-logging and damping off. The pot just a fraction larger will usually provide ample space.

To turn out the pot, one hand should be spread over the top of the soil holding the stem between the fingers, and then the pot inverted. If necessary, the root ball can be given a push with a pencil through the drainage hole so it will slip out. The drainage material must be removed and, with gentle pinching and rubbing motions, the soil ball reduced until it is small enough to go into a clean pot. There should be 1 inch of clearance between the cleaned ball of earth and the side of the new pot. Adequate drainage is achieved by covering the hole on the bottom of the pot with a piece of broken flower pot, concave side downwards, and covering this in turn with a layer of flower pot chips or gravel. A layer of moss on top of this will prevent fine soil sifting through and clogging drainage.

A little moist compost should be put into the pot

When plant roots run around the inside of the pot, then it is time to pot on the plant into a larger pot. Crocks and gravel must be placed in the bottom and, as the soil containing the roots is now smaller than the pot, fresh compost should be added firmly around the sides

and pressed down lightly. Any damaged roots should be cut off with the sharpest knife available. Roots may be cut back in moderation to induce fresh growth and if the plant is an awkward shape it may be lightly pruned. The soil mark on the stem indicates the level for planting and as the soil settles the plant will sink to a slightly lower level. A potting stick is helpful for working the compost down the sides of the pot. The top soil should be evened up and the plant watered thoroughly and then not again until the soil has almost dried out.

Propagation by division is the simplest method of vegetative propagation and one of the easiest. It should be carried out under clean, hygienic conditions with clean tools and hands and the plant material chosen for propagation should be healthy and vigorous. The plant should be knocked out of its pot, the roots freed of surplus soil, gently pulled apart and singled out each with a separate stem, leaf or crown, and removed with a sharp knife, with roots attached. Each division is potted as a separate plant in a suitable sized pot using a good growing

Separating the rhizomes of an old *Aspidistra* to make two or more plants

(Top) young plants are produced on the lower leaves of *Tolmiea menziesii* where they touch the soil. *(Below)* *Saxifraga sarmentosa* produces shooting runners

compost. It must be firmed, watered and placed in a propagating frame with light shade until growing strongly, when it can be grown on in the conditions suitable for it as a house plant.

Soil-layering can be used very satisfactorily for plants with trailing stems, or low shoots that can be easily bent down. With house plants it is used chiefly for plants that produce stolons or runners, with small plantlets on them, the plantlets being inserted in small pots placed beside the parent plant, firmed and pegged down. They are not severed until rooted. For soil-layering shoots, the method is slightly different. Robust young shoots are chosen and the sap flow partially interrupted just beneath a node, or bud, by sharply bending the shoot or making a slanting cut halfway through the stem. This part of the shoot must be bent, inserted into a pot filled with moist compost and pegged down. It helps to dust the cut area with a hormone rooting powder. The soil must be watered regularly and rooting may take place several months before the layer is ready to be severed and to be grown on alone.

Stages in air-layering

Air-layering is practised on shoots that cannot be bent down easily, and is useful for propagating overgrown plants, such as *Ficus elastica*. A narrow ring of bark is removed below a suitably placed bud on the stem, or a slanting upward cut made halfway through the stem. Any leaves are detached, the area treated with rooting powder and then a large handful of moss, moistened with a dilute solution of hormone preparation, wrapped around the stem to enclose the cut, and enclosed in polythene. When white roots can be seen penetrating freely through the moss, the layer can be severed, the polythene removed and the rooted portion potted up.

Parts of a living plant severed from it, to be rooted and grown as separate but identical specimens, are termed cuttings. It is best to root cuttings in a balanced compost in which the roots will be well established before being transplanted. **Stem cuttings** are usually taken from the ends of young robust shoots, in active growth. The shoots must be cut cleanly with

African violet leaves rooting in water

Propagating soft cuttings

Propagation from *Begonia rex* leaf

a sharp knife and, in the case of very soft-tissued plants, the cuttings should lie for a few hours to let the cut surface dry off. The cuttings should be stripped of their lower leaves, firmly inserted in the rooting medium for about half their length and lightly sprayed with water before covering with glass or polythene.

Leaf cuttings are taken for the propagation of fleshy-leaved plants and succulents. A mature adult leaf with stalk can be inserted in the rooting medium with the blade of the leaf just above the surface. Plantlets develop at the base of the stalks and can be transplanted as soon as they are easily handled. The leaves of African violets may be rooted in a jar of water. Propagating by leaf cuttings is also used for large leaves with prominent veins, especially *Begonia rex*. A firm mature leaf should be selected and the main veins cut through just below where they divide on the underside. The leaf is laid, right side up, on the surface of the rooting medium and anchored flat with the help of small stones or bent pins over the main veins. Small plantlets grow from the cuts and they can be separated when they are large enough to handle.

Cleaning and protecting house plants

Plant foliage in the home collects dust just as the furniture does and, apart from making the plants look dirty, it impairs leaf functions and periodically should be removed by sponging or spraying. Large-leaved plants can be cleaned by wiping the leaves with a sponge, or soft cloth, dipped in soft water. A little milk added to the water gives them a soft sheen, and any oil or grease on leaves can be removed by adding a few drops of vinegar to the water. A supporting hand should be put under the leaves as they are wiped to avoid any risk of damage and, whether they are cleaned with tepid water, soft soap and water, milk, skimmed milk, white oil emulsion or furniture polish, is a matter of choice. Oil has the advantage of acting as a pesticide against red spider, because it prevents the red spider moving around to feed. A weak mixture is advisable, not more than one dessertspoon to a gallon of water, otherwise the leaves may suffer as the oil will clog the pores a little and attract further dust. The plant must be kept in the shade until it is dry. Fine-leaved plants can be

Neanthe bella, the smallest of all palms. Sponging is beneficial to most plants

cleansed by close spraying with a mist sprayer but plants with hairy or downy leaves, cacti and succulents, can be more effectively freed from dust with a fine camel-hair brush. Fallen foliage and dying flowers should be promptly removed, the surface soil lightly pricked over when necessary and moss growth removed.

House plants rarely suffer attack from insect pests, especially if the plants are given proper care and attention, examined about once a week and cleaned occasionally. However, sometimes one is unlucky enough to obtain a plant that is already infected, or to find that pests have invaded from outside. Infestation can usually be effectively controlled, if action is taken immediately pests are seen, usually by using lethal insecticides. It is, nevertheless, wise to remove an infested plant from the room to prevent any spread of infestation and also to carry out treatment. This should be done, either out of doors or in a well-ventilated room or cellar, where insecticides can be used without harming household furniture or upsetting humans or pets.

Insect pests: 1. Ants can loosen roots if in sufficient numbers; 2. Scale Insects frequently infect ivy; 3. Aphids on a tender shoot of *Cissus antarctica*; 4. Mealy Bug

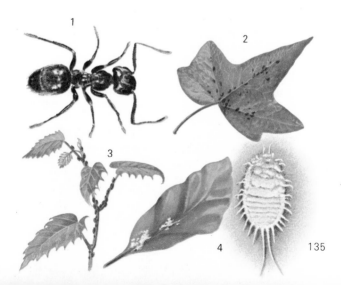

The tender shoots of *Gynura sarmentosa* are vulnerable to greenfly

Dilute white spirit and cotton wool on a toothpick used to deal with Mealy Bug

The following descriptions are of pests that an owner of house plants may, on some occasions, be unlucky enough to find. Descriptions and methods of treatment are also included.

Ants are only likely to encroach from the garden if they have access to a fairly large area of dry sandy soil. They can cause much damage to roots and can be eradicated by dusting the soil with special powders.

Aphids attack all parts of the plant and seriously damage the tissues by sucking the juices from them. Colonies of these 'greenfly' can sometimes be eradicated by hand, otherwise they must be sprayed with an insecticide, paying strict attention to the manufacturer's instructions and applying it as a fine mist from a small syringe.

Mealy Bug is a slow-moving insidious pest, which is covered with a mealy wax so that colonies of them look like small pieces of cotton wool. Under the protection of this covering they suck the sap from the leaves of the plant. The plants should be sponged with a spray-strength solution of a white oil emulsion, or the colonies dabbed with a swab of cotton wool on the end of a matchstick dipped in methylated spirit.

Red Spider feed in very large numbers on the undersides of the leaves of a wide range of plants, causing considerable debilitation and damage. The symptoms are yellow mottlings with a greyish cast on the upper surface of the leaf which in extreme cases will wither and drop off. They are barely visible to the unaided eye but an ordinary magnifying glass will show them up quite clearly. Spraying with liquid derris, persistently, at ten day intervals is an excellent non-poisonous remedy. They usually occur when conditions are warm and dry.

Scale Insects are strangely immobile insects that attach themselves like small brown limpets to the shoots and undersides of the leaves of plants. Syringing with an insecticide two or three times at ten day intervals is a good remedy but, for plants with large leaves, sponging with a spray-strength solution is probably a better method.

Thrips or blackflies are tiny, dark brown insects which attack both leaves and petals in large numbers causing much damage. Insecticides or spraying with a soft-soap solution will control them.

White Flies are readily recognized as a rule as small white flies on the undersides of leaves and damage plants by sucking the sap. They are susceptible to insecticides and in plant rooms the growing of a few plants of African Marigolds has a deterrent effect.

African marigolds discourage White Fly

ARRANGEMENTS OF HOUSE PLANTS

Wardian cases and terrariums

Just over a hundred years ago Dr Nathaniel Ward, a London physician, discovered that plants could be grown in sealed glass containers and his discovery, helped by his invention of the Wardian case, made it possible to grow green foliage plants in a Victorian drawing room with a minimum of trouble. By present-day standards these were somewhat ornate and heavy in design, but the principle is excellent today. The moisture is transpired from the leaves and being unable to escape into the atmosphere, condenses on the inside of the glass and runs back down into the soil, then again becomes available for the use of the roots, in a sort of perpetual motion cycle. These sealed glass cases were originally invented by Dr Ward as a means of transporting exotic plants on long sea voyages. Needing no attention in transit, it was a successful method, and was later adapted for Victorian drawing rooms. There seems to be no reason why one should not be constructed in an alcove, or corner, perhaps in conjunction with artificial light.

Small aquariums with a base of slate cut to fit the floor and some small pieces of water-worn rock placed on top of the soil make good fern cases; using young ferns less than 2 inches high if possible. When planted with the ferns, the 'garden' can be sprayed thoroughly, a piece of glass, cut to fit, placed on top and then left undisturbed for some months. When it appears to be dry the top can be lifted off, the fine spraying repeated and the top replaced.

Terrariums are also easy to look after and again watering is cut to a minimum. The sides should be lined with moss for about a third of their height and then a base of charcoal should be put on the bottom, followed by 1 inch of gravel and a layer of soil mixture. Two parts loam, two parts coarse sand, one part leaf-mould is a suitable medium. The largest and tallest plants should be put at the back, the smallest at the front. The glass lid of the terrarium should be removed for a few hours if water condenses inside. It should be placed in a good light, but not strong sunlight. Plants suitable for growing in terrariums are winter-flowering begonias, *Fittonia, Helxine,* miniature ivies, *Maranta,* palms, *Peperomia* and saintpaulias.

A modern Wardian case with artificial lighting. The half shelf enables a number of plants to be displayed and a metal tray of moist gravel provides humidity

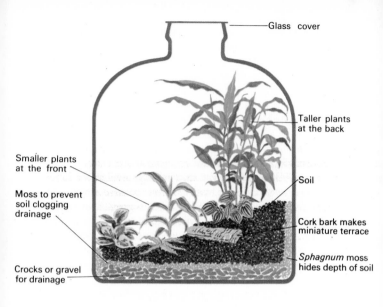

Glass cover

Taller plants at the back

Smaller plants at the front

Soil

Moss to prevent soil clogging drainage

Cork bark makes miniature terrace

Sphagnum moss hides depth of soil

Crocks or gravel for drainage

The plants in the section through a bottle garden are *(from left to right)* Peperomia, Cryptanthus, Dracaena, Peperomia sandersii and Codiaeum

Bottle gardens

An extension of the Wardian case idea is the use of large acid or water bottles, known as carboys, for growing plants arranged as small gardens. The bottle must be washed with strong detergent, rinsed well with clean water and allowed to dry thoroughly before planting. A soil mixture should be made, consisting of two parts loam, one part peat, and one part coarse sand, with a little charcoal added. It must be mixed well and placed in the bottom of the carboy by means of a funnel of thick paper. As the plants will not need to make much growth, no fertilizer is necessary. After the arrangement of the plants has been decided, they should be gently pressed through the neck of the bottle and allowed to fall on the soil beneath. The actual planting is best done with the aid of two smooth pieces of wood, 2 feet 6 inches long by $\frac{3}{4}$ inch wide and $\frac{1}{4}$ inch thick. A light watering through a long-spouted watering can will settle them in after planting. If the top is sealed no further watering will be required, if left open, watering will be required occasionally, but it must be done with the greatest possible care. The bottle is an original feature of a room, and can be easily converted into a lamp.

A planted up bottle garden. In the foreground is *Selaginella* a moss-like plant allied to ferns, *Maranta leuconeura massangeana (left).* In the centre is *Dracaena godseffiana* with *Anthurium scherzerianum (right).* At the back is *Dizygotheca elegantissima.* The plants in this display will not increase much more in size.

141

Dish gardens

Dish gardens can be bought ready made from the florist, but they are apt to be cluttered up with too many wishing wells, bridges, foolish plastic figures, pagodas and other gimcracks. It is certainly possible for anyone with a little bit of artistic skill, and perhaps with none at all, to be able to get more satisfaction from a home-made product, as well as the pleasure that comes from the actual assembling; the joy of actual creation.

Arrangements of this kind are usually ephemeral, their length of life depending largely upon the sort of plants used and their culture. Plants that are taken from the woods and, for example, then kept in a dry room with a high winter temperature cannot be expected to last for ever. It is inevitable also that some plants will grow more quickly than others, so that the scale and balance of the composition is upset. Even so, an arrangement of living plants is much more lasting than an

A dish garden arrangement of *Dieffenbachia*, an ivy, *Cryptanthus* and primroses. When the primrose flowers fade they can easily be replaced by another small flowering plant.

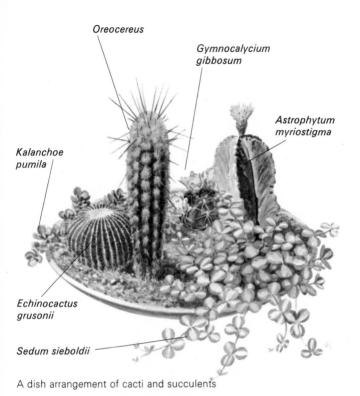

Oreocereus

Gymnocalycium
gibbosum

Astrophytum
myriostigma

Kalanchoe
pumila

Echinocactus
grusonii

Sedum sieboldii

A dish arrangement of cacti and succulents

arrangement of cut flowers, and the fact that it does not last
for ever does mean that there is an excuse for a change in form.
Receptacles, too, can be as varied as the plant arrangements
that they contain. Almost any fairly shallow container about
4 inches deep will do for the dish garden and it can be made
of pottery, wood, wicker, china or metal providing that
whatever is chosen has drainage holes in the bottom to allow
surplus water to escape.

If a dish with drainage holes is not readily available, or a
particular one is especially wanted for a display, then ample
drainage material must be relied on. The dish must then also
be given an exceptionally porous soil and careful watering to
avoid water-logging. Drainage material can consist of broken
flower pots, charcoal broken into $\frac{1}{2}$ inch pieces or even smaller,

coarse sand, fine gravel and cinders or clinkers of a suitable size. To prevent the soil from immediately sifting into the drainage material, and this is particularly important when using water-tight containers, moss, which can be obtained from any woods, will provide a temporary barrier between the soil and the drainage material, although the soil should be inspected at regular intervals to see that the drainage material is not becoming clogged.

The character of the soil does not matter very much for these arrangements and anything that can be moistened to keep the roots from drying will do, because it is known in advance that they will only be transitory plants. For a general selection of plants, a mixture of equal parts of sand, loam and well soaked peat will be very suitable, with the addition of another part of broken charcoal for arrangements that

Making a dish garden: The drainage material should first be placed in the selected pan and should be composed of gravel, small pieces of charcoal and clinkers or crocks. Plants are removed from their pots and placed where desired and compost sifted between the plants to settle the dish firmly

consist of cacti and succulents.

Additions to the display above ground can include such accessories as small rocks of pleasing form and colour, and more especially those which have lichens growing on them. Pieces of bark, odd shapes of dead wood, or beautiful mosses can also be included in suitable arrangements.

An arrangement of cacti and succulents is very suitable for a dish garden, especially for a hot dry room. There is such a variety of both from which to choose, that it is possible to make a very varied and interesting picture. Specialist nurseries can supply particular plants in a variety of form and colour and shops sell many more popular species. These cacti and succulents are grown mainly for the beauty of their stems, spines and leaves but sometimes they give their owner an extra bonus of flowers, often very brilliantly coloured.

(Below) a dish garden for a cool position in the house. The plant *(right)* is *Grevillea robusta*, one of the hardiest of house plants. The fern is the Hart's Tongue Fern and the violets add colour. Decoration is provided by the mossy stone and the piece of bark. The violets can be replaced when they have finished flowering

Bonsai

The literal meaning of the word 'bonsai' is 'planted in a tray' and refers to the attempt to artifically perfect natural tree forms in miniature. A recent trend is to plant a number of trees in a group and produce a miniature forest, or to plant trees and shrubs around rocks to give an impression of plant life on rocky terrain.

Bonsai can be grown from seed, collected from nature, or cuttings rooted. Adequate watering, sunshine, fertilizing and suitable soil are necessary and with careful pruning,

(Below) a winter-flowering Jasmine, 15 years old and 1 foot high

(Above) three Japanese Maples in winter, with leaf buds forming, 10 years old and 1 foot high

trimming, wiring and repotting, miniature growth is finally accomplished. These processes, however, require specialist knowledge and much practice and, for most household requirements, it is better to buy already established plants.

Because the amount of soil is very limited, Bonsai require frequent watering and this should be done when the top of the soil is still slightly damp. The amount, of course, varies with the seasons and trees require more water during periods of active growth. Spraying the leaves in hot weather is also essential.

In general, a small amount of fertilizer should be given in

spring and a larger amount in the autumn. Liquid nutrients have to be applied frequently and it is better to place a non-liquid form on the soil surface, where it will break down gradually.

Sunshine and fresh air are essential if the trees are to remain healthy and spraying with an insecticide and/or fungicide regularly, as directed, will increase general protection. Some of the more tender species must be kept indoors during the winter, as well as young trees, deciduous trees with thin branches, trees in very shallow pans or on rocks and trees

Chinese Juniper, 200
years old and about 30
inches high

that flower or fruit during the winter season.

Repotting must be done when roots begin to crowd one another. The roots can be loosened and some removed. The correct amount of fresh soil can then be replaced.

Ideally, bonsai should appear aged, yet with fresh foliage. Proper potting and feeding will keep this appearance and new buds should be trimmed off occasionally to prevent the branches from growing and thickening. Withering may occur if the branches are badly trimmed.

Mixed bowls of house plants

A bowl, trough or some other container planted up with a selection of house plants can be very attractive, whether it is composed of flowering house plants, or of foliage house plants, or a mixture of the two. The different plants must, however, be selected with some care. Obviously it is necessary to choose plants that require similar conditions of soil, light and temperature as well as plants that will look good together.

Once again the ideal container is one that is provided with drainage holes and, if it is to stand on a piece of furniture, it should be given a plate or metal tray on which to stand. It is often possible to find a brass or copper bowl with short feet which can be given an additional false bottom of perforated zinc. This will prevent root-rot caused by water-logging, especially if the bottom of the bowl under the zinc is lined with polythene cut to shape. The polythene should be allowed to come up the sides of the bowl for about $\frac{1}{2}$ inch. A good handful of granulated charcoal placed at the bottom of the bowl will help to prevent the compost from getting sour.

Ficus elastica doescheri

In the front the plants are *(from left to right)* Dieffenbachia, *Primula obconica* and *Tradescantia blossfeldiana tricolor*

Kalanchoe

At the back is *Cordyline terminalis* and in front *Begonia rex (left)* and *Fittonia argyroneura*

A good seed compost can be used for filling the bowl and it will benefit by the addition of some granulated peat, one part to every two to three parts of compost, depending on the plants in question. It is important to soak and squeeze out the peat before it is used, otherwise it will absorb all the moisture from the compost. A rich compost is not needed during the early stages of growth and feeding should only take place after the plants have rooted well into the compost.

The planting up of a bowl needs planning ahead. Plants may look suitable companions at first, but if one is a more vigorous grower than the others it will quickly swamp the other plants. It is, of course, possible to prune a vigorous plant back, but vigorous growth denotes vigorous root action and less active plants may well be starved of essential nutrients.

The dwarf specimen of the Poinsettia, *Euphorbia pulcherrima,* *(above)* forms the focusing point of this Christmas bowl. The other plants in the bowl are *Philodendron scandens, Hedra helix variegata, Chlorophytum* and *Pilea cadieri.* The red bracts of the Poinsettia should remain on the plant for at least three months. Then the plant can be replaced by another plant that would provide a splash of colour, such as a *Primula* or a hyacinth.

The small Cocos Palm *(opposite)* dominates the small bowl. The bold leaves of *Spathiphyllum* are a good contrast on the left. Two pepperomias occupy the centre front; these are *Peperomia hederaefolia* and *Peperomia magnoliaefolia.* The spotted plant is Croton, the two creeping plants are *Pellionia pulchra* on the left and *Ficus pumila* on the right. The display is further enhanced by pieces of attractive bark.

However, a little forethought will prevent any difficulties and there are an enormous number of possible combinations. During the Christmas season many bowls of house plants are made up and offered for sale. These look most attractive especially when perhaps a cyclamen has been added or one or two hyacinth bulbs are in flower. The foliage plants will out-live the flowering plant and bulbs but they can be removed in due course and another house plant substituted.

A good mixture of coloured foliage plants for a bowl would be *Gynura sarmentosa*, *Hedera canariensis*, Croton, *Rhoicissus rhoimboidea*, *Cryptanthus fosterianus*, *Tradescantia tricolour* and *Cryptanthus tricolor*. For a trough, the height of plants must be remembered and taken into consideration. Too many plants of similar height are seldom effective. *Ficus hycata*, *Hedera* 'Glacier', *Hedera* 'Chicago' and *Begonia rex,* are suitable for an assorted height, foliage-filled trough. Another, longer trough could consist of *Ficus tricolor*, *Dracaena*, *Scindapsus* 'Marble Queen', *Peperomia magnoliaefolia*, *Aphelandra*, *Maranta*, *Hedera* 'Green Ripple' and *Citrus mitis*. A large pottery bowl with a stem will look most attractive and important if filled with *Scindapsus* 'Marble Queen' on a moss stick and *Begonia Rex* and *Philodendron imbe* 'Red Burgundy' around the base; particularly if the bowl is dark grey or black, for it will enhance the colours of the foliages.

Zebrina purpusii

GLOSSARY

A few of the less common terms used in plant descriptions, and not fully described within the text

Acute: ending in a point; sharp
Adnate: joined to another organ or part
Alternate: of leaves, arranged in two rows but not opposite or spirally; not more than one at a node
Annual: completing its life cycle in one year from germination
Axil: angle formed by junction of leaf and stem
Axillary: arising in the axil
Berry: a fleshy fruit which does not open, containing seeds, without a true stone surrounding them
Biennial: completing its life cycle within two years; growing the first year, flowering, fruiting and dying the second
Bisexual: hermaphrodite; having both stamens and pistils in the same flower
Blade: the expanded part of a leaf or petal
Bract: a modified leaf growing near the calyx of a flower
Calcifuge: lime-intolerant; of plants usually found growing in soils free of calcium carbonate
Calyx: the sepals, or outer leaves forming flower cup
Campanulate: bell-shaped
Chlorophyll: the green colouring matter of plants
Compressed: flattened
Cordate: heart-shaped
Corm: a short, swollen underground stem, the next year's development occurring close to the old one
Corolla: the petals of a flower as a whole

Corymb: a cluster of stalked flowers arising from different levels but making a flat-topped head

Crenate: having shallowly rounded or convex edges

Cyme: a branching inflorescence where the central flower opens first with lateral branches that also have terminal flowers

Deciduous: dropping off; of plants losing leaves annually

Dentate: toothed

Digitate: fingered; shaped like an open hand

Elliptical: about twice as long as wide

Elongate: lengthened out

Entire: of leaves, not cut or toothed

Ephiphyte: a plant growing on another but obtaining no nutrient from it, hence **epiphytic**

Evergreen: of plants retaining their green foliage for at least a year, throughout their dormant or rest period

Falcate: sickle-shaped

Filament: the stalk of the anther

Fimbriate: with the margin finely divided into a fringe

Florets: small individual flowers, particularly those in the heads of Compositae

Fungus (pl. fungi): plants without chlorophyll

Genus (pl. Genera): a group of species with common characteristics

Glabrous: without hairs

Glaucous: blue-green 'bloom' on the surface

Half-hardy: of plants requiring protection from low temperatures

Herbaceous: of plants, which do not form a woody stem

Hybrid: a plant arising from the fertilization of one species by another

Inflorescence: the flowering stem above the last leaves

Internode: the part of the stem between two nodes

Keel: sharp edge in leaf formation; lower petal or petals, shaped like a boat, of flowers

Labiate: lipped

Lanceolate: lance- or spear-shaped

Lateral: on, or at, the side

Linear: long and narrow, with sides almost parallel

Lobed: divided by indentation but not separated

Node: joint; part of stem from which leaves arise

Oblong: of leaves longer than broad

Obovate: inversely ovate

Obtuse: blunted, rounded

Orbicular: rounded

Oval: tapering evenly to both ends

Ovate: egg-shaped, with broad end nearest the leaf stalk

Palmate: usually of leaves with more than three leaflets arising from a common point

Panicle: a branching raceme

Pedicel: a stalk of a single flower

Perennial: living for more than two years, normally flowering each year

Petal: a separate leaf of the corolla, usually coloured

Petiole: the stalk of the leaf

Pinnate: having leaflets in two rows on each side of a stalk

Pinnatifid: pinnately cut but not fully divided

Pistil: the ovule and seed-bearing organ

Procumbent: lying loosely, flat on the surface

Prostrate: lying closely along the surface of the ground

Raceme: a simple, unbranched inflorescence, hence **racemose**

Radical: of leaves, arising from ground level

Receptacle: the upper part of the stem from which the flowers arise

Recurving: bending backwards in a curve

Reflexed: abruptly bent backward or downward

Rhizome: an underground stem lasting more than one year

Runner: a special shoot forming a new plant at the end

Rugose: wrinkled

Sagittate: arrow-shaped

Seed: a fertilized and ripened ovule

Sepal: one of the separate green leaves of a calyx

Serrate: saw-toothed, hence **serrated**

Sessile: without a stalk

Shrub: a woody plant, branching freely from the base

Simple: of leaves, not compound

Sinuate: having a wavy outline

Spadix: a fleshy inflorescence

Spathe: a bract enclosing one or a number of flowers

Species: a group of individuals with constant characteristics

Spike: an inflorescence with flowers sessile on an unbranched axis

Stamen: the male reproductive organ of a plant

Stem: the main axis of a plant

Sterile: incapable of reproduction

Stolon: a creeping stem of short life tending to root production

Tendril: an organ sensitive to contact by which some plants grasp supports and climb

Terminal: borne at the end of a stem or branch

Tuber: a swollen portion of an underground stem

Tunic: a dry, usually brown covering round a bulb or corm, hence **tunicated**

Umbel: an inflorescence in which the flower stalks all arise from the top of the main stem, giving an umbrella-shaped head

Undulate: wavy

Vein: of leaves, a strand of strengthening, conducting tissue, sometimes called a nerve or rib

Viscid: sticky

Whorl: a group of similar plant parts arising in a ring at the same level

Xerophyte: a plant able to live where there is little water

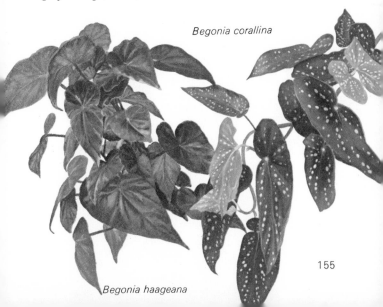

Begonia corallina

Begonia haageana

BOOKS TO READ

The following books are useful aids to the growth, care and recognition of many house plants. They are usually available from bookshops and public libraries.

Be Your Own Houseplant Expert by Hessayon. Pan Britannica Industries Ltd.

Cacti and Succulents translated by E. E. Kemp. Studio Vista, London, 1963.

Greenhouse Plants by Ilford Colour books. Ebury Press, London.

House-plants by Margaret E. Jones. Penguin, Harmondsworth.

House Plants by Ilford Colour books. Ebury Press, London.

House Plants by A. J. Huxley. Amateur Gardening Handbook, Collingridge, London, 1964.

House Plants by Edward Hyams and George Elbert. Thomas Nelson, London, 1967.

Illustrated Encyclopedia of House Plants by Violet Stevenson. Pearson, London, 1965.

Indoor Plants by Xenia Field. Hamlyn, London, 1967.

The Master's Book of Bonsai by the Directors of the Japan Bonsai Association. Collingridge, London, 1968.

On the Growth of Plants in Closely Glazed Cases by N. B. Ward. 1842.

The Rochford Book of House Plants by T. Rochford and Richard Gorer. Faber, London, 1961.

INDEX

SOME OTHER TITLES IN THIS SERIES

■ **Arts**
Antique Furniture/Architecture/Art Nouveau for Collectors/Clocks and Watches/Glass for Collectors/Jewellery/Musical Instruments/Porcelain/Pottery/Silver for Collectors/Victoriana

■ **Domestic Animals and Pets**
Budgerigars/Cats/Dog Care/Dogs/Horses and Ponies/Pet Birds/Pets for Children/Tropical Freshwater Aquaria/Tropical Marine Aquaria

■ **Domestic Science**
Flower Arranging

■ **Gardening**
Chrysanthemums/Garden Flowers/Garden Shrubs/House Plants/Plants for Small Gardens/Roses

■ **General Information**
Aircraft/Arms and Armour/Coins and Medals/Espionage/Flags/Fortune Telling/Freshwater Fishing/Guns/Military Uniforms/Motor Boats and Boating/National Costumes of the world/Orders and Decorations/Rockets and Missiles/Sailing/Sailing Ships and Sailing Craft/Sea Fishing/Trains/Veteran and Vintage Cars/Warships

■ **History and Mythology**
Age of Shakespeare/Archaeology/Discovery of: Africa/The American West/Australia/Japan/North America/South America/Great Land Battles/Great Naval Battles/Myths and Legends of: Africa/Ancient Egypt/Ancient Greece/Ancient Rome/India/The South Seas/Witchcraft and Black Magic

■ **Natural History**
The Animal Kingdom/Animals of Australia and New Zealand/Animals of Southern Asia/Bird Behaviour/Birds of Prey/Butterflies/Evolution of Life/Fishes of the world/Fossil Man/A Guide to the Seashore/Life in the Sea/Mammals of the world/Monkeys and Apes/Natural History Collecting/The Plant Kingdom/Prehistoric Animals/Seabirds/Seashells/Snakes of the world/Trees of the world/Tropical Birds/Wild Cats

■ **Popular Science**
Astronomy/Atomic Energy/Chemistry/Computers at Work/The Earth/Electricity/Electronics/Exploring the Planets/Heredity/The Human Body/Mathematics/Microscopes and Microscopic Life/Physics/Psychology/Undersea Exploration/The Weather Guide